John Brookes
Garden Design Course

John Brookes
Garden Design Course

MITCHELL BEAZLEY

John Brookes Garden Design Course
by John Brookes

First published in Great Britain in 2007 by
Mitchell Beazley, an imprint of Octopus Publishing
Group Ltd, 2-4 Heron Quays, London E14 4JP

Created and produced for Mitchell Beazley
by The Bridgewater Book Company Ltd.

Creative Director: Peter Bridgewater
Project Editor: Stephanie Evans
Project Designer: Andrew Milne
Picture Research: Liz Eddison
Illustrations: Simon Rodway, Andrew Milne

A CIP catalogue record for this book is available
from the British Library

ISBN 13: 978 1 84533 299 0
ISBN 10: 1 84533 299 7

Set in Interstate

Printed and bound by Toppan Printing Company
in China

Contents

3 Context & Technique

4 The Design Process

5 Specialities

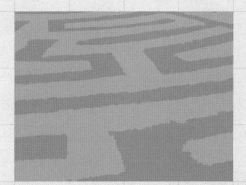

6 Frequently Asked Questions

1 Introduction

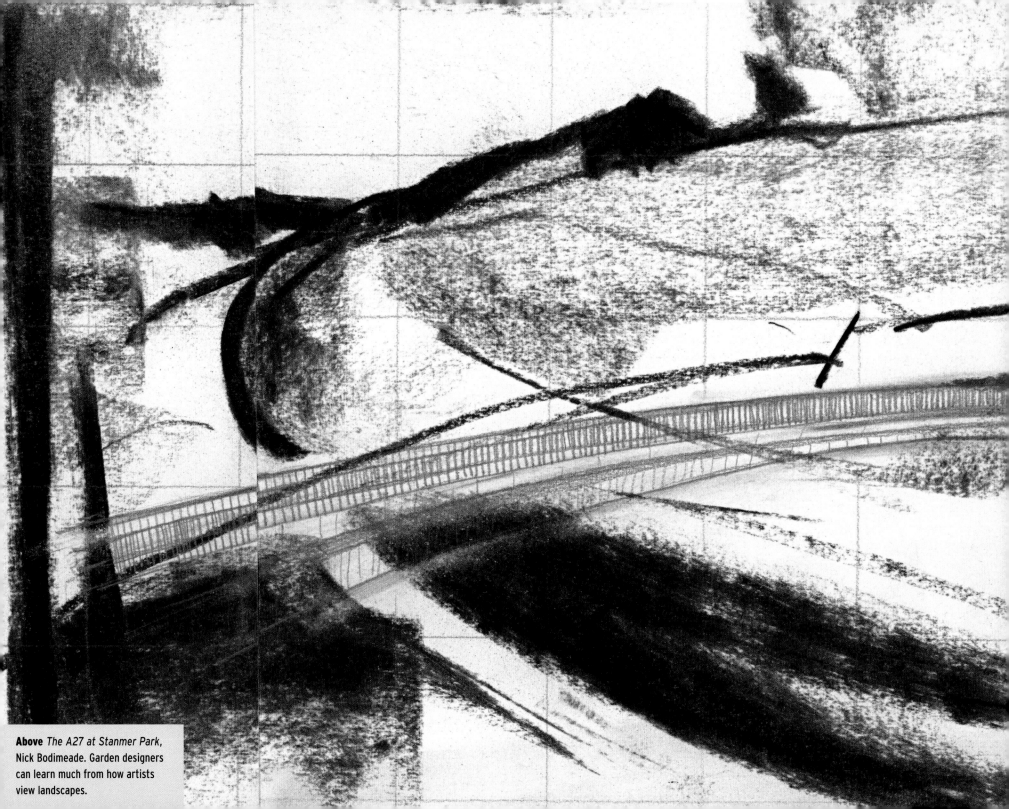

Above *The A27 at Stanmer Park,* Nick Bodimeade. Garden designers can learn much from how artists view landscapes.

"Our lifestyles have changed and our houses have changed, but that stuff beneath our feet has not. We need to tread carefully for we are only the caretakers of it for a very short period."

Our perception of what a garden is constantly changes. The concept with which I grew up was that it was a place to grow decorative plants and vegetables. I was part of the tail end of a period when the main garden design criteria were to grow exotic and half-hardy plants and to produce as much colour as possible. I was born the year after Gertrude Jekyll died, and her influence was paramount throughout the middle part of the 20th century. She was in fact an early conservationist and, following her mentor William Robinson, she 'pooh-poohed' exoticism and instead extolled the virtues of temperate perennials and woody plants grown in elegant and time-consuming borders. She also advocated a concern for the local idiom, its style and its materials. Her example was followed and interpreted by Edna Walling in Australia, and in America by a number of lady gardeners including Beatrix Farrand, who also worked in Britain, at Dartington Hall, Devon.

These were essentially plants-people, who painted their often beautiful pictures into a plan that was imposed upon the garden environment, for they worked within a large and affluent social landscape. Today, at the beginning of the 21st century, we are increasingly adopting a stance that we are not superior to nature, and forcing a plan upon it, but that we are part of it and are becoming more and more sensitive to it.

Since World War II, the twists and turns in garden design have been subject to the twists and turns of society's progress. The modern lack of garden maintenance skills was key to reducing the 'grand garden' in scale and complexity. The emergence of large suburban areas surrounding our cities has also been an important factor in the changing face of gardening: large numbers of houses with gardens whose owners' concerns go beyond growing fine plants to include sport and leisure.

Latterly, in downtown city areas there has been huge interest in small-space usage on the ground or on the roof, where new materials and techniques are being used to create a mood that could not be called horticultural at all. On the other hand, the demand for allotment space in which to grow one's own produce is enormous. At the same time, small-scale downtown public landscapes provide possibly some of the more interesting developments in garden design.

However, our early interest in the environment has subsequently turned into a concern for it. Many previously uninterested potential gardeners wish to create an urban or suburban paradise for birds, butterflies and small mammals and, as a result, planting techniques based upon regional growing patterns have emerged – re-creating the meadow, the steppe and the prairie.

The media has tracked this horticultural journey to an extent – donning Miss Jekyll's muddy boots, though pandering too often to the requirements of the small screen to provide entertainment.

Slowly, with increasing improvements in design across the board, we have seen an emergent new profession: the garden designer (by which I mean a professional person who has experienced the breadth of vision and wide discussion that only a degree in the subject can supply), a role which has begun to influence the way we see the garden now.

Environment, art and design

Early in the 20th century artists began to break away from the restrictions of gallery spaces, which led to a development in what was first called earth art, followed by land art and now environmental art. The concern of these movements is the use of space and its medium, meaning whatever material is available on site. This is far removed from the horticultural exoticism of the past and will take garden design into new realms of abstraction, with a closer identification of each and every site.

So the techniques of garden design are no longer necessarily initialised by a horticultural interest – new influences from travel, a multi-cultural society and individual experience all begin to shape and refocus the way we see our gardens in their setting.

This very 'specialness' of individual places does not necessarily support international modernism, which swept through the design world of the 1920s and 30s and which tried to apply a universal vocabulary of form and colour. The vocabulary is fine, but its application can now be too strident, I believe. Though I would defend to the death the healthiness of the modernist movement, in some north temperate climates, for instance, it simply did not work. Constantly fed modernity from sunnier latitudes, gardeners back home strove to reproduce it, causing a tension between the new and the old. I wonder whether there isn't a way to develop a modern garden far closer to nature, to its rhythms and patterns, than has been previously attempted? The lessons of previous styles and fashions are never lost, for we filter our current thoughts through them, using something from here and something from there, and this is called progress.

One can develop or reclaim a neglected space, moving on from traditional conservationism and instead innovate in ways that extend existing links and relations. We need to take account of the aesthetics of a place – culture and horticulture – and blend them through design into a new forward-looking solution, albeit one based on a more ancient narrative.

We are constantly pressurised to embrace the new but we should realise that the old has done us pretty well. Our lifestyles have changed and our houses too, but the stuff beneath our feet has not. We need to tread carefully for we are only the caretakers of it for a very short period. Over the centuries our landscape (and it is within this context that the garden designer works) has withstood various forms of farming, mineral extraction, houses and cities and many tons of industrial waste. And yet it is still a beautiful place – albeit now endangered, and never more so than as a result of global warming.

It is into the midst of this environment that the garden designer has to evolve his or her plot, no matter how minuscule it might be. The architect and the developer must listen, the local planner, the parish clerk too: the landscape designer (a new hybrid) could lead.

"We need to take account of the aesthetics of a place... and blend them through design into a new forward-looking solution, albeit one based upon a more ancient narrative."

Below There is a new American look, of which Oehme & Van Sweden are masters, using perennials and grasses, which considers organic materials both practically and sculpturally. Designers can encompass all these features according to what the client wants.

Why design a garden?

Many designed objects through the 20th century seemed unnecessarily different in both function and fabric and for a long time a designer not concerned with something as practical as engineering seemed a bit odd. Well, things have changed. The idea of designing anything no longer seems frightening. We now have designer clothes, designer interiors and kitchens and indeed whole designer lifestyles can be created, so why not designer gardens?

You may well have discovered that putting together all the gadgetry of a modest kitchen is far more difficult than evolving the concept with space, and it is no different outside. As garden spaces become smaller, and we demand more of them, fed by summer holidays abroad, as well as all the ads for decks, outside furniture, jacuzzis, plunge pools, pizza ovens – let alone anything to do with growing plants – many people find that they just don't know where to start. On the other hand, as owners of larger gardens get older they need things simplified and made easier to maintain. Alternatively, we may just want a revamp.

What is garden design?

Design is to do with logic and suitability and, increasingly, sustainability. Style, of course, comes into it too, as well as cost. So the design process is a sequential step-by-step reasoning of where it is, who you and yours are, and what you want, and then making all these elements fit together within the space.

This does require some technical drafting ability – although nothing arty – to get your idea on paper and to scale. You may have made cut-outs of furniture before and moved them around in a room to try a new layout. Well, you can do exactly the same in a garden but on a plan, providing areas of grass, paving, water and planting. The main differences are the scale on which you are working and that you have to think ahead as well. Consider who will look after these living plant things. Don't forget that they have a habit of growing too. So design helps you to project your ideas into the future, as well as helping you to plan for the daily, or weekly running of the space.

Envisaging the look

Yes, a garden can be a bind if you have a busy lifestyle but it can also be a hugely restful addition to your routine. How well you design your space will ensure that you get the garden you want and one you can look after. Sometimes, as I potter in my own garden, visitors say "What a chore!" or "Rather you than me!" But I think "You poor souls, you haven't got it" – by which I mean the satisfaction of envisaging the future look that you are trying to create or design in your mind's eye and then watching it grow. Gardening is a total 'switch-off' from everything else and, for me, designing is the same. To bring the two together in one concept is very fortunate indeed.

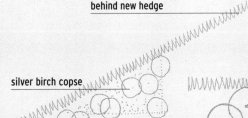

tool shed, rubbish, etc
behind new hedge

silver birch copse

seat

swimming pool

shrubs

conservatory

house

dustbins

garage

shrubs

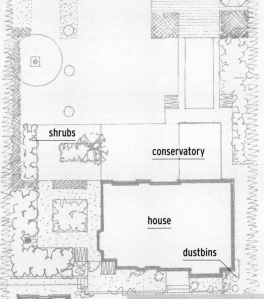

Above Context, proportion, and scale
are important elements to get right.
If the underlying design works (for that
is the most enduring part of the plan) the
plant material, the decorative element, can
be introduced gradually to fit the space.

"Gardening is a total switch off from everything
else, and for me designing is the same.
To bring the two together in one concept is
very fortunate indeed."

Left and above Gardens mean different
things to different people, of course, and
it is the designer's job to ensure that – no
matter how large or small – the space is
functional, practical, and pleasant to look at.

How we see gardens

I am lucky to be able to design gardens in all manner of places and this has made me realise how very differently people feel about their gardens. Generally, temperature affects not only what grows but how we use the space outside and as my great guru Thomas Church wrote: "gardens are for people". Obviously, in a warm climate you do more outside – eating, swimming, sunbathing. And this need makes for a greater fluidity in house design as well, an interaction between inside and out. Shade, too, is important and water is vital for growing anything. So, as lifestyles, buildings and usage differ with climate, so does plant material.

The harsher the climate, the more it is necessary for the gardener to use native plant material, it being better adapted to its own climate and probable lack of water – the cactus and the succulent, moist palms, for instance, broadly define a very hot climate. The climate around the Mediterranean, in South Africa and similar latitudes in Argentina, Chile, California and in parts of Australia tend to provide a broader palette of plant material and those of us who live at comparatively sun-starved latitudes tend to head to these places on holiday. We often view them as the ideal and want to recreate the same back home, seeing the garden as an escape, or continuation of our holiday. In trying to grow exotic plant material we perpetuate the 19th-century ideal of excellence in horticulture rather than being too aware of the 'look' that we create. I am not advocating the use of only native material, though certainly a knowledge of what grows locally (if it were allowed) is helpful – rather the need to create an eye for 'suitability'.

Location, location, location

What is suitability? 'Appropriate' may be a better word, but what is appropriate and what is mere fashion? Is the prairie look appropriate in town, for instance? No, it is not, but on the other hand prairie techniques of planting and, to a degree, plant selection can loosen up the look of the Edwardian border, which is equally inappropriate on either a small scale or if labour is at a premium.

Above right The practicalities of climate will of course dictate the range of plants that can be used. The look of a desert garden is quite strong and architectural by the nature of its drought-resistant flora.

Below right A Mediterranean climate engenders another equally strong range of plant material. The more testing the climate the more the plant has to adapt to its rigours.

More appropriate in northern latitudes is the meadow look, if you have the space and your garden is open; better still, I believe, is learning from nature – the natural way of using material in your area. You can observe it in local woodland, for instance, or on the heath or at the edge of the recreation ground, if the maintenance of these areas has not relied too heavily upon chemicals.

Slowly I am edging towards the new appropriateness or suitability for locations. This is an idea that works not only when thinking about plant material but also when considering building materials and building styles. It would be wonderful to create that colourful Mexican adobe look, but would it cheer up a wet winter's day or merely cause deep depression? Again, it might be appropriate in some places – it's entirely to do with suitability for its location.

Sustainability, however, is always appropriate and is the current buzz-word in our globally-warming world. How do you create, maintain and sustain a garden without damaging the delicate ecosystem in which it sits through the use of chemicals? It is important to maintain the fertility of the ground organically, and to ensure the retention of as much moisture as possible by using mulches and helping the soil by incorporating water-holding organic material.

Nature's palette
'Environment' is another word used a lot. What does it mean to the gardener or garden designer? It means having a care for the area in which the garden sits. The sum total of our gardens is a huge chunk of the environment. Increasingly, gardeners are interested in the wildlife their gardens attract – birds, bees and

"Slowly I am edging towards the new appropriateness or suitability for locations."

butterflies. Those in rural situations have wildlife in the form of rabbits and deer thrust upon them. "What can I grow?" the gardener wails. The answer is to look around and see what the wildlife leaves alone and learn from it. In woods near my garden are early bulbs (probably escapees), ferns, bluebells, wood anemones, rhododendrons, and foxgloves galore. To these add box, yew, viburnum, whitebeam, and you will see that nature's palette should not be ignored.

The way in which we see our gardens has changed hugely. The garden used to be a sanctuary from nature, but increasingly the new garden can provide a sanctuary for it – tamed and doctored to size and suitability, of course.

Top right The English climate, being soft and benign, lends itself to a look that is generally small leafed and soft coloured, and not far removed from the cottage garden idyll.

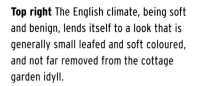

Gardens are for people – and places

We are so conditioned to think in horticultural terms, that the first thing a new gardener does is to buy plants. You wouldn't dream of introducing a new baby to a household without making any nursery preparations, and it's the same with plants: both are living things, and both need nurseries.

Unless you are growing for production, plants are in fact only the decorative element of a garden. A much more fundamental element in its design is how the space works for you and your family, and whether you live in an urban environment, the leafy suburbs or the countryside, the garden becomes a transition into your surroundings and it is sometimes what you remove, not add, that defines this continuity. In reverse, looking towards your house it's the treatment of the surroundings, both hard (buildings and structures) and soft (plants, shrubs, trees and grass), that binds the house into its site.

From within your home it is important to consider its surroundings for every month of the year. Remember that you may not use the garden very much at all unless you live in a hot climate; consider also that it serves as your approach to the property, a vital means of access for pedestrians, cars, deliveries and trash collection, along with storage, of course. Then there is access around the property and around the garden itself. Is the terrace wide enough for entertaining and is it sufficiently shady in summer? If you have a swimming pool, is there space for changing, and is the surface surrounding the pool non-slip? Do you wish to add a barbecue, or a jacuzzi – all features that make the space more enjoyable for people.

Whether you are building a garden, or modifying an older one, you will discover that local materials are the cheapest. But is the local stone or chippings the wrong colour for your concept? Suddenly, you are considering the styling of your layout in relation to both the house it surrounds, and in some cases the landscape beyond. So the basic 'cut' of the garden, or its design, is what makes the thing work for those who live in it and manage it. It is so important to get the foundation right: planting will not disguise a badly designed garden or one that has not been designed at all. Your plants should be the final icing on the cake.

The remarkable differences in the requirements for a garden are highlighted by the fact that one hardly ever sees two the same. The permutations of homes, their orientations, sites and the families who live in them are immense. There is a huge difference between a small urban garden for a non-gardening, young family with pets, and a larger suburban or rural garden for a couple who were once active gardeners but have now retired and are feeling the strain of mowing and hoeing. With forethought it is possible to design a garden that can be adjusted – vegetables becoming lawn, sandpit becoming pond, and so on – but few manage the transition, and statistics show that many do not remain in one place long enough to see such changes through.

> "Unless you are growing for production, plants are in fact only the decorative element of a garden."

Left At the end of the day, whatever the season this activity in the garden is to me heaven! And gardens should be designed for this activity.

Right Other gardens will be viewed as spaces for children to use and play in – these activities are not incompatible if designed into the concept.

The role of a designer

So where does the garden or landscape designer fit into all of this, and just what is the difference between a landscape architect, a landscape designer and a garden designer? It's worth defining the different roles, because sometimes I find myself explaining: "I am a garden designer - not a magician."

A Landscape Architect is a member of a professional body (such as the American Society of Landscape Architects in the United States or the Landscape Institute in Britain), whose training has ranged over a far greater spectrum of public and social spaces than that of private gardens. Having said that, many landscape architects are splendid garden designers. Plants-people may suggest that their knowledge of garden plant material is weak – though they may well be very strong on environmental and native plantings.

The Landscape Designer's brief might be wider than that of the garden designer, but he or she is not into planning issues or civic design work and is instead concerned with an awareness of the surroundings and landscape, usually in small parks and larger gardens or estates. The landscape designer has usually been a garden designer, and has sought out this particular field of interest.

The Garden Designer works in the context of the domestic garden. Increasingly he or she is a professional who has completed a degree course or equivalent vocational-type qualification, is a member of a professional society (such as the Society of Garden Designers in Britain or the Association of Professional Landscape Designers in the US) and is a competent professional. I would add that, obviously, newly graduated students (unless they have previous training) will not have a vast spectrum of knowledge about plant material at their fingertips – that takes years to amass – but will have up-to-date expertise on construction methods.

Turning ideas into reality

Being a garden designer is a tricky job and different clients will use their designer in different ways. Additionally, different designers have different expertise. Ideally, if you wish to commission a garden designer, you would seek them out through personal recommendations, then by checking on his or her website, and by visiting a garden they have developed. Finally, you should then meet and talk with him or her. Before such a meeting it is essential to decide what it is you want. Your designer will want to work with you on this and it is his or her job to transpose your ideas (with some of their own) into a reality.

Here I speak personally. While I am happy to work within a budget, I do not want such considerations rammed down my throat. If the work the client envisages has structure in it (say of a terrace, a pergola or a pool), it is the designer's job to propose the best solutions. Once that is resolved, the next step is to decide how the structure is built and with what material. Remember: the variable to sort out initially with the client is the design solution, not the budget. The next stage is to think about the planting in detail. Of course, there may be no structural design required at all – for instance, the terrace is large enough, the pergola looks fine and you've made your own pool – but if what you need is a planting designer to help with the next phase, do ensure you like their work.

Then again, you may want to do it all yourself. This book will help. You have to interpret the instructions, of course, but you will get the sequence of how to think about each element of a garden and then progress to making it.

> **"the variable to sort out initially with the client is the design solution, not the budget."**

Left This prize-winning garden design by Andy Sturgeon, M.S.G., at London's Chelsea Flower Show shows how the concept of the garden is being influenced by the sculpture, but all is softened with plant material.

Far left Hardy shrubs and bricked steps with a formal seating area are hallmarks of the early 20th-century architect and garden designer Edwin Lutyens, whose influence is apparent in many English country houses.

2 Elements of Good Design

Who is it for?

There is a remarkable difference in the requirements of a garden space, which is indicated by the fact that one hardly ever sees two gardens the same. The permutations of houses, their orientation, site and the families who use them are immense. Compare a small urban garden for a non-gardening young family with pets, and the larger suburban or rural garden for a once gardening couple, now retired and feeling the strain of mowing and hoeing. Both scenarios are common enough, and the difference between them is huge. These two families need to swap places, and indeed this often happens.

With forethought it is possible to design a garden that can be adjusted to the stage in life – the vegetable plot becoming lawn, the sandpit a pond and so on – but few manage the transition, and the statistics show that we don't remain in the same dwelling long enough now to ring those changes. Instead what it comes down to is that the person who maintains the garden takes the decisions as to what it is for!

Increasingly, the secluded space of a private garden becomes the safest place in which children can play. And on a small scale, children's play and intensive gardening do not go together – so throughout the early years of a family the space has to be given over to activity.

Hard surfaces on which to tricycle in a circuit are desirable, though with no right-angled corners. A place to kick a ball about takes over from the cycle stage, and then a teenage space in which to sunbathe or install a jacuzzi.

If the family can be persuaded to eat together, it will be at the barbecue or pizza oven, again requiring hard surface and plenty of space for partying. Suddenly night lighting is needed and one really sees that the garden has become another room – fully used in summer, and intermittently in winter.

But what of the planting in such a room? Many now see the garden in warm weather only in terms of their holiday experiences in the Bahamas, Florida, Turkey or Spain. So the demand is increasingly for exotics, which

accounts for the abundance of phormium (New Zealand flax) and cordylines (New Zealand cabbage trees). Stronger perennial colours are back in fashion and the good old dahlia tops the list again, along with agapanthas. Most of these plants can be grown in tubs or pots and the range available is huge.

Larger suburban or rural gardens will want all the above, but to the list one can add the swimming pool and the tennis court. For the fastidious, the sort of garden I am describing can be fairly time-consuming, and involves huge amounts of clearing up. Storage space is vital.

With all this work the larger garden owner wants to cut down on the traditional chores of mowing and cultivating. Here the use of longer grass requiring less maintenance can be useful. There can be attractive mown paths through the rough areas, which may contain fruit trees, with bulbs beneath them for spring colour and even wild flowers, given the correct conditions. But someone has to do it all – and that is the crunch!

Younger gardeners are getting increasingly interested in organic food and in growing their own vegetables. Those who have a small urban garden given over to outside living may seek out an allotment and travel quite long distances to get to them. The modern requirements have changed from those of the traditional allotment holder: no longer does one see acres of cabbages and rows of potatoes, but instead a selected few named varieties of the latter in pots, along with a limited range of more specialist vegetables and herbs.

Left Pared back to its barest minimum, a garden is a place of one's own but it does not require boundaries or plants to achieve that. Here the focus is on creating a space from which to experience what lies beyond.

Right Gardens can, of course, be our retreat from the wider world. A garden can be very therapeutic, provided, of course, the design allows that its maintenance is manageable, rather than sheer hard work.

What is it for?

For the embryo garden designer some sort of checklist to follow on site is a good idea. If sent in advance to a prospective client it allows them to sort out what is wanted. This tactic also negates family members squabbling in front of you – hopefully. For the designer, I forgot to say earlier, is sometimes called in to adjudicate between man and wife and their wishes for the garden. So huge tact may be necessary.

This analysis of the site and its requirements is equally important if you are doing the job for yourself, possibly even more so, since we tend to be indecisive when it's our own problem.

Use the sample form opposite as a basis for obtaining the details you require. Armed with this information you will then have parameters within which to work.

Above Many gardens evolved piecemeal with bits added on by a succession of owners. The designer must rationalise the space, accommodating the mundane along with the aesthetic requirements.

Sample briefing form

Client's name/general information

Address

Number in family
Children, and their ages
Older people

Their interests
Pets and numbers

Type of house

What the client wants
Terrace – both sun and shade
Late evening sun in summer
See distant view/Obscure an unsightly feature
Block wind or noise
A few vegetables, in small raised beds
Herbs
Raspberry cage
Dry access around garden
Small greenhouse, and standing ground for pots
Carport area
Lawn
Shrubs and ground cover
As low maintenance as possible

You will eventually add to this

Location

Local vegetation/seen from the car

e.g. oak/ash
pine/birch
open/heath
woodland/coastal

Soil

by observation and what's growing
pH value - roughly

Orientation of site

N, S, W, E

Drainage

any obvious damp places

Building materials

house - stone, brick, slate, tile

Boundaries

wall, fence, woodland, and so on.

Right The demands made on any space will vary greatly according to the occupants. With experience, observation, and by asking the right questions you can quickly identify what the design needs to achieve.

Scenario 1

The immense pressure on space in Japan's cities mean that most urban dwellers' homes are compact – but many have gardens too. For this family, an outdoor room has been created in which to entertain family and friends.

Scenario 2

Front gardens serve a different purpose. Access is paramount and most people want to present a well-ordered approach to their homes. The requirement here was for a low-maintenance frontage, which is achieved by extending the paved areas across the width of the house, rather than simply building a uniform flight of steps to the door.

Scenario 3
Rather than compete with
the tranquil scene beyond
this North American garden,
the gentle reflections of this
watery landscape are repeated
in the design of the foreground
formal pool.

Where is it?

There was a time when gardening publications never showed a structure in a garden shot because it would give away the property's location, which meant that burglars could not see how to gain unobtrusive access through windows and doors, but it also meant that the garden was not telling you where it was. Things may have changed now, but even if a shot doesn't show the minutiae of a building, its location should be seen to set the mood for the garden around it.

Within this broad parameter are differing geographic or climatic zones, and within each one there are gardens by the sea, gardens in mountains, woodland gardens, wetland gardens, and so on. For it is climate that really dictates the interaction of house with garden and how the garden will be used.

We often assume that sunlight is the factor that makes a garden work, but even in the northern hemisphere, where sunshine is at a premium, it should be remembered that many older people do not need the sun and younger people should take heed about protection from it. I was initially surprised at how strong the sun can be in the United States and Canada at certain times of the year. For people with second homes in the sun or in many locations south of the equator, shade is really vital. In the Middle East, for example, pools may need to be covered in order to protect the heads of swimmers.

Wind is another factor to consider, nowhere more so than by the sea. Walls are needed, perhaps with 'open' work to filter the wind in hot places. Elsewhere, shelterbelts should be suggested long before anything decorative is attempted.

Celebrating the indigenous

The location of the garden gives a clue to its styling as well. I have been involved with a garden in the Caribbean where the house architects used a Polynesian style, with Polynesian and even African decoration. Both locations may share the same temperature, even the same plants or the same lifestyle, but such an incongruous style does not work. The indigenous Caribbean vernacular is loud, colourful and very different from the Polynesian equivalent.

The celebration of what is particular to a local environment is morally important if we are not to disappear in the 'gloop' of global corporate culture. Each region of every country has a language, both in planting and vernacular terms. By all means, the designer can alter, modernise (since vernacular is too often muddled with old-world charm) and adapt, but let us leave Japanese gardens in Japan and Spanish ones in Spain. The discretion of Japanese style can be emulated and the joy and splash of Spain reinterpreted, but do it in a manner that does not jar with your site or with me, your visitor.

Left The nature of the surrounding countryside and the agricultural practices of an area should give clues as to what will 'work' in the garden context. Look at the hedgerows, the farm buildings, and what is growing by the side of the road for guidance.

> **"...a point overlooked is the importance of the view of the garden from inside the house."**

The view from within

Wherever the garden is located, a point frequently overlooked is the importance of the view of the garden from inside the house – seen when sitting down, when standing in your kitchen, or from your bedroom window, for instance. So the designer needs to get into the house to experience how for themselves how the garden is viewed, while at the same time discreetly observing the home's interior colours and décor, and ultimately how the client's garden could relate to the interior. Sliding doors or a French window naturally help this interaction and flow of space, and the smaller the area the more important this becomes. You may also see from inside how the garden can form a transitional sequence from house to terrace, garden to surroundings, where applicable. So as well as planning for use, one has to plan for how the garden looks from inside as well as outside.

Top right Gardens are as appreciated from within as well as without, especially in latitudes where at certain times of the day or year it is too cool, or hot, to be outside.

Right Not all gardens are about growing plants. There are many scenarios in which the requirement is simply for somewhere to be part of the wider picture.

Context

Some people have an eye for analysing a site and are able to explore and exploit the local idiom; others have to work at it. Artists have recorded landscapes and buildings since time immemorial, but we also have the camera, traditional or digital, and I believe that using one or both can help to focus the eye. After all, I suspect we would all like to create a garden that a professional photographer would wish to capture, but what is it that makes a good composition – a few years after the garden has been designed?

To help understand the aesthetics of a place, try this design exercise. Arm yourself with a sketchpad and a digital camera and try to capture the broad landscape (or townscape) of the area around you, paying particular attention to its shapes and landforms. Close in on older buildings, such as barns, churches or even factories. Then focus on the walls and fences, gateways and any other specific details of the area. Now look at local (native) planting – weeds if they are in the wrong place. They may be at the side of the road, in a local wood or on an old building site. See their beauty. Explore the variety of leaf shapes and textures, and the range of flower colours. All these forms, shapes and colours can be made into a collage to illustrate the region in which you live.

Learning the language of design

If you don't know much about your local area, you can do a bit of research in your nearest library. Is there a local stone and what is its content? What type of wood is used to make fences? You can also undertake some hedgerow analysis. Use this research to add details and names to the content of your photos and sketches. Next, look at a small-scale map, even an aerial photograph of your area, to see what you can deduce from the shapes of fields and field names.

Even if none of this comes to play in your garden design, you have started to look around and begun to learn the visual language of design, and hopefully be interested in shape. For that is what a garden plan is all about: shape and proportion – the shape of the lawn, the planting areas, perhaps a water feature. When designing a garden, you make up a patchwork or collage of shapes, which should be functional as well as aesthetically pleasing. This collage becomes the basis of your garden plan. And if these shapes can have a relationship to something outside your site, as well as to the materials with which you build, you are linking your building into its site. This, in my view, is the ideal.

Opposite Observing the immediate vicinity is the obvious starting point for both understanding and learning from the local idiom. Successful garden designs are, I believe, in tune with their surroundings.

Above Devon Field I by Linda Looker, a view that is stripped down to the bare essentials – here, the red soils of a hillside. As designers, we can learn a great deal from the 'eye' of others.

"...what is it that makes a good composition – a few years after we have designed it?"

Opposite The understated simplicity of this garden reflects the style of a South American house and its coastal setting.

This page The profusion of planting in this garden in Virginia looks natural, precisely because its creators have observed what grows best in the surrounding locality. It pays to resist introducing exotics, which only jar with the visual language of a place.

Pattern

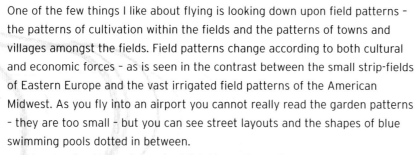

One of the few things I like about flying is looking down upon field patterns - the patterns of cultivation within the fields and the patterns of towns and villages amongst the fields. Field patterns change according to both cultural and economic forces - as is seen in the contrast between the small strip-fields of Eastern Europe and the vast irrigated field patterns of the American Midwest. As you fly into an airport you cannot really read the garden patterns - they are too small - but you can see street layouts and the shapes of blue swimming pools dotted in between.

I love seeing these shapes and it is the pattern of shapes within a garden that I enjoy looking for, as well as creating and evolving them myself through my work. So often one sees beautifully planted gardens, full of wonderful specimens, but without any ground pattern to hold them together, and that is a very important part of garden design. Once you start looking at pattern, you see it everywhere - man- or machine-made - and not necessarily a repeated pattern as in a tartan fabric; the pattern can read as an entity in itself. It is the pattern of a garden that holds your eye and which leads you to look at an internal feature, perhaps, or to the view beyond.

It is the job of the garden designer to reconcile various shapes in a garden and this is achieved using pattern. The challenge may be how to introduce a piano-shaped swimming pool into a triangular site with a rectangular house or merely how to make a long, thin garden attractive. The skill is in how you define the pattern using the scale of its parts.

Below Pattern can be seen in everything, once you know how to look for it, both incidentally and deliberately in our man-made world and in nature; think of sand dunes, clouds, leaf forms or snowflakes.

Right Artists interpret patterns in nature: the grain of wood, the contours of a slope, or channels in a river bed. I encourage students to draw curves to help them 'loosen up' in their design interpretations.

Shape

The shapes that make up the pattern affect the overall effect of the layout. For instance, the shapes in a formal and balanced pattern will be strict and regular, creating a classic, symmetrical layout. Such a collection of shapes might suit the layout of a strictly formal house such as a Georgian or colonial-style dwelling. However, broadly speaking, we lead less 'strict' lives today and the design of our living spaces reflects this. This means that, in designing a garden, while the shapes you evolve may be regular, they can be employed in an abstract way to create an asymmetrical layout. By regular I do not mean only straight. Curves can be geometrical or flowing. I think that curves should still employ a geometry in their conception rather than be free-shaped wiggles. That may be personal preference but there are practical reasons too, paramount among them being maintenance, and ease of construction, depending upon the material of which they are made.

Increasingly, maintenance and the machinery employed to fulfil a function dictate the shapes. Ride-on mowers, for instance, like to move in a continuous curving pattern, while mechanical carriers prefer a straight and sweeping path. Tight angles are difficult if not impossible to negotiate.

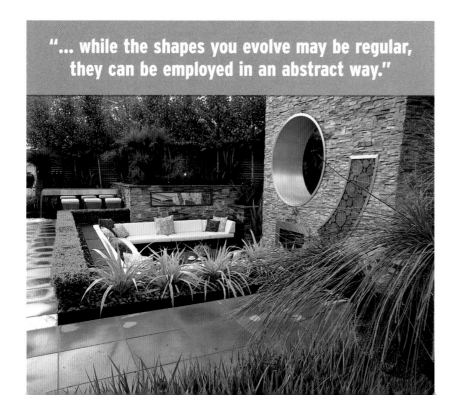

"... while the shapes you evolve may be regular, they can be employed in an abstract way."

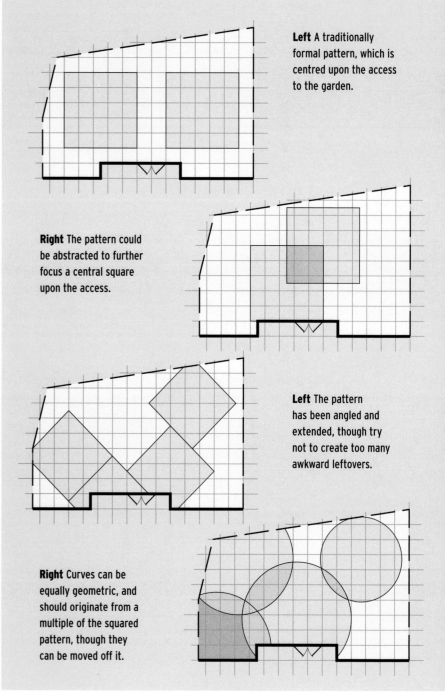

Left A traditionally formal pattern, which is centred upon the access to the garden.

Right The pattern could be abstracted to further focus a central square upon the access.

Left The pattern has been angled and extended, though try not to create too many awkward leftovers.

Right Curves can be equally geometric, and should originate from a multiple of the squared pattern, though they can be moved off it.

This page It is far easier to see the key shapes when they are traced out on overlay. That way, you begin to see the layout for a design. The formal, symmetrical shape may be more immediate, but even more natural, flowing curves can have a geometric logic.

Scale

Scale
I have taken a basic overall pattern and enlarged it somewhat in the centre. The bottom shape is really only a small section of the overall. Start looking at pattern in the abstract and play with its geometries.

Using scale is one way of making the connection between the garden and its site. Many people have large trees at the bottom of their garden or nearby. The masses – the sizes of areas and objects in your garden, such as the length of the lawn, the width of your planting, the breadth of your pond, and so on – should relate to the scale of these trees. We tend to play safe and make things small (or, even worse, cute), but your scaled concepts should be bold and simple. You can do this by enlarging a detail and by losing some of the content of a design.

This idea of relating the scale should be carried through to the dimensions of details in the garden, such as the width of a border against the height of a fence or hedge, for instance. The width of the border needs to be the same as or wider than the height of such a boundary to create a sense of generosity in the design. On the other hand, a small-scale design tends to focus the eye within the site. This works well if there really is nothing eye-catching beyond the garden, but where there is a view or a key feature, such a design would just get in the way of the bigger picture.

I shall discuss how you make a design fit its site in due course, but once you get the hang of it, you can turn your design around on the page, or within the site, without losing the proportions. You can also 'fracture' your proportionate design, by breaking apart shapes or details, provided you can still 'read' how the design would fit together again. The extent to which the design is retained will depend on the scale of the pattern and the scale of the fracture. If the fracture is too narrow, there is no point and if it is too wide, you lose the connection.

Right A simple formal pattern interpreted into a garden layout. Note the softening effect of plant material.

Above An Andy Sturgeon design at Chelsea which moves the pattern at an angle to the site. The shape of the pavilion and seat relate to each other.

Proportion

What we are now talking about is a proportionate relationship between different elements of the two-dimensional garden plan.

Most of us, I suspect, would 'read' what we call a balanced or symmetrical pattern, which might ultimately produce a formal garden. Its proportions would be pretty straightforward where the shapes seem logical and symmetric within a layout. But it is surprising how very few contemporary sites lend themselves to such rigid formality these days. There's always a garage or a bay window, which upsets the symmetry. And in any case, they are pretty boring. An asymmetrical pattern, while being more difficult to balance, that is to get its proportions correct, can produce a much more exciting garden plan.

In the accompanying exercise I have indicated three balanced and proportionate drawings, which you might imagine as pictures on a wall. Now lay the wall flat to become a garden plan (the proportions change of course) and start to play with those shapes to retain pleasing proportions. Use a bit of colour perhaps and you are starting to think about the proportions of a basic garden layout without any knowledge of where it is, or for whom - simply its pattern.

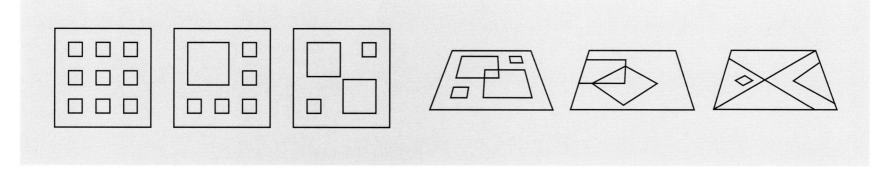

Opposite The new planting of gravel areas with grasses. The treatment is particularly suited to this garden in Argentina, where the pampa dominates. This is a garden form of the pampa, designed by Barzi & Casares.

Above These sets of drawings illustrate not only patterns you can create with, in the first three, say, pictures on a wall, but also the importance of the space between them. It is a proportionate relationship and is no less important if you place the patterns on the ground. The next three images show how you can abstract those shapes to become garden plans. The shapes define areas of lawn, water, paving, etc. - the elements of good design.

Above top The curving shapes of these bench seats 'talk to one another' across the intervening proportionate space. This garden is another one by designers Barzi & Casares.

Masses & voids

The next step in evolving from a two-dimensional plan into a practical and usable tool is the introduction of the third dimension – height – into your design, considering the concept of (eventual) masses and voids (the spaces between the masses). Now we begin to exploit the full potential of the site.

Then the height you decide to introduce might be structural: a raised bed or a sunken area (depth, as it happens), steps or retaining walls across an uneven area, though we are not there yet! In fact, the type of mass you must consider first is the height and girth to which your plants will eventually grow. (Note that it is only at this stage that plants begin to put in an appearance.) This consideration highlights the fourth dimension – time – which few other art forms, for that is what we are practising, have to consider. So, by giving height to areas of your flat plan, you begin to see how they can relate to their surround.

Very simply, you can prepare scaled elevated sections across your site, or you can turn your plan round and start to project the height upwards to give an idea of your masses, say, five years' hence (see below). (In the garden, five years seem to go in a flash.) At this stage, think of these masses only as plant material, like clipped box or yew, though in your mind's eye you will be envisaging them as functional components of the design: shrubs, perennials, ground cover, and so on.

Alternatively, you can use a CAD program to project your plan upwards so that you can start to see a view away from the house, and even back towards it (see opposite). But you will also notice the spaces between the masses: the width of the terrace against the house, how your plan relates to the height of trees beyond the garden, and so on. You are starting to think in three-, even four-dimensions. You will begin to see that if the void between the masses is too great, they lose their relationship – though if you heighten the masses it works again, provided the increased height is bulky enough to be proportionate with the intervening void.

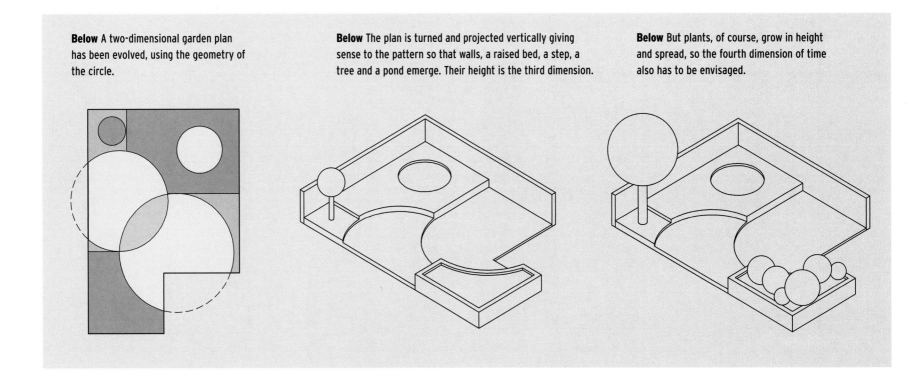

Below A two-dimensional garden plan has been evolved, using the geometry of the circle.

Below The plan is turned and projected vertically giving sense to the pattern so that walls, a raised bed, a step, a tree and a pond emerge. Their height is the third dimension.

Below But plants, of course, grow in height and spread, so the fourth dimension of time also has to be envisaged.

Using CAD to resolve masses & voids

Drafting with CAD is far quicker than hand drafting because repeated elements only need to be drawn once and then copied, scaled, or rotated. This is especially helpful when drawing elements that are more complex or when you are trying out different ideas to resolve a design. For masses and voids, for example, where the challenge is to balance the planted (masses) and the open (voids) spaces of lawn, ground cover, gravel, or a patio, CAD drafting has specific tools, including multiple copying and hatching patterns, to quickly fill an area.

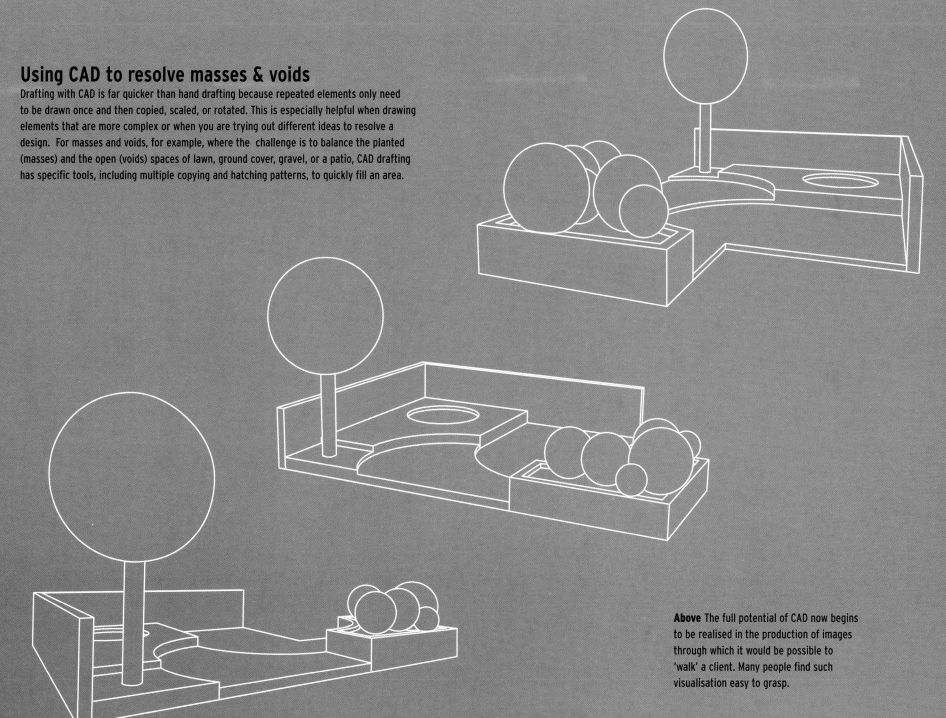

Above The full potential of CAD now begins to be realised in the production of images through which it would be possible to 'walk' a client. Many people find such visualisation easy to grasp.

Above left When evolving a planting detail, you can quickly prepare a sketch of the shape and mass of your projected concept. This gives an instant summary of your masses and voids.

Above centre Or, used more architecturally in relation to a building, once you know how to read the masses and voids, you can see very clearly how your space and height are going to work out.

Right Exactly what these structures are, I do not know – but you can very clearly see how masses and voids are being considered, and then contrasted with mop-headed trees.

Above This feature has a strong dynamic, which is arresting, in terms of the choice of material in an otherwise rural context. It commands the attention, and encourages us to descend the steps.

Dynamics

The types of pattern that you evolve in your garden – and then prove when they are transposed to a third dimension – can be restful, or they can be strong. This dynamic also helps to relate your pattern to its site.

On a small scale, for instance, the garden dynamic will probably be inward-looking, ending with a feature to hold the eye in the site, as in a town garden. Where a feature is apparent beyond the site, the aim of the pattern should be to lead the eye towards that outside feature, be it a mountain, a valley, a church spire or a single, magnificent tree, perhaps using another feature within the garden space as a counterpoise. If you are lucky enough to have a good view from the garden, your pattern should make full use of it – though, perversely, too wide a horizon is difficult to take in and it perhaps needs breaking and/or framing.

Structuring the space

You may, then, wish to create 'rooms' with your pattern, so that a walk through the garden becomes a pleasant meander from one space to another. There was a time when vistas and perspective were talked about, but this terminology rather reeks of gracious living, and 18th-century rural landscapes. Although plenty of landscapes still evolve on this scale we would now describe the approach to designing them differently.

There are those who still prefer a meticulous formal layout, which might well match the house and the owner's lifestyle, but such formality usually requires precise maintenance. By contrast, a wild garden, you might think, is just a mass of plant material with no lines or patterns. The wild garden that appeals to the eye, however, usually does have a structure and logic to its design, otherwise it becomes chaotic, but the lines and shapes are covered with plant material. Most of us settle for a garden somewhere between extreme formality and the wild.

Remember also that the size of a design should be for the convenience of the user, as well as to create a visually satisfying composition, both from the house looking out and from outside the garden's boundaries looking back towards the house; it is a two-way thing.

"The types of pattern that you evolve in your garden... can be restful, or they can be strong."

Above The dynamic you create in your garden determines the way it is perceived. A restful dynamic slows the pace, allowing for distractions, whereas a strong dynamic encourages direction and purpose.

Plants

'But where do the plants come into it?', I hear the horticulturally tuned cry. Of course, plants are the decorative material and help to style your pattern but they also serve to infill the pattern to create privacy and/or shelter, and to flesh out the pattern, giving it bulk or mass.

To a degree, certain patterns in a garden go with certain styles of house – formal with classic, rambly with cottage and so on. Then there are various national styles of pattern: we can pick out a French, Japanese, or Spanish garden for instance. It is the selection of plant material that often defines the style more than any other element.

Thanks to the Gulf Stream, Britain's balmy climate enables plants from around the world to be grown, and the nation's gardeners can create styles of garden with more or less appropriate plant material. There are not many other places on earth I have discovered that have this same luxury.

Because I am an English designer when I work abroad I am often asked to create the 'British look', which, if one has to rely on plant material, is almost impossible to do. After much trial and error 'the look' that people seem to like, is one achieved almost by lack of maintenance back home – one where plants sprawl about, self-seed and pop up where not asked for – but over a generous and strong layout. It's that winning combination of Lutyens and Jekyll working together – good design and a generous planting overlay. It has little to do with exoticism, and increasingly more to do with suitability for the particular site.

The Lutyens–Jekyll stricture can be applied to any form of design in any place – it all goes back to scale, line and proportion. (The contemporary working duo might be Gustafson and Oudolf.) The dynamics of plant selection are part of this satisfactory styling.

"It's that winning combination of Lutyens and Jekyll working together – good design and a generous planting overlay."

The fashion trends

At the beginning of the 20th century, colour and rusticity seemed to be the optimum – with exoticism as a leftover from the Victorian garden to show off the gardener's cultivation skills. As the century progressed, plant selection gradually became more and more important. With the trend towards modernism in architecture and design (a movement that was not concerned with gardens), plant selection too tended towards the architectural: the spiky plant, the vertical accent, the horizontal layered plant, the rounded shrub rose look. This architectural movement probably reached its limit with the flower arranger's selection of plant material, which became very sophisticated. We then seemed to slant to a French provincial look: box-edged beds with lavender or white rose infill. Herbs were popular on the one hand and formal topiary on the other, reflecting a split in style preferences.

The herbal wellbeing school moved through to thinking of environmental issues, while the formal school still seems nuts on topiary everywhere, though the environmentally concerned start to think about native plants, and then, more ecologically still, about habitat and plant association.

Left The look of my own garden is one that I am often asked to replicate. Before embarking on the planting, I will consider suitability for the location, rather than an 'off-the-peg' solution.

Below left Rusticity has moved on to embrace naturalness, combined with environmental concern.

Right The Arts & Crafts movement fostered a desire for rusticity where it was not always appropriate. This thatched garden house with its surrounding flower garden appears totally pleasing, however.

Plant association

This is a new philosophy of planting design, which can quickly depart from horticulture to become land management. The theory of placing plants within an association still has merit – particularly when the newcomer is trying to distil this wilder concept down to a smaller garden scale. The eyecatcher, punctuation, repetition, even layering, are all techniques worth studying.

The eyecatcher This is a plant that says 'look at me'. The horticulturalist, in pursuit of growing, will fill his space with too many eyecatchers, which grab the attention when seen in mail-order catalogues but create an unrestful plant association: the too-blue conical conifer, the purple *Prunus*, too much variegation (though I like a little). Gold foliage is anathema to some people, but used generously in a dull northern climate I think can look great. So it may be to do with an inappropriate shape (lollipop, for instance); it may be the foliage or even flower colour (though this tends to be transitory).

Repetition If a plant is worth using in your space repeat it and not just once, plant in larger groups. Even in a small space you are working against the scale of the boundary wall, or a neighbour's tree – usually something large, so think about the proportion of your groupings to these heights. Use fewer plants and you are back to their becoming an uneasy eyecatcher. I know it is hard to buy in groups at a garden centre, but before making an impulse buy, try to resolve your planting on paper and you will see the number you need.

By repeating a plant group across or down a garden space you steady the design concept down. When you repeat a few groupings over and over again you create a calmness to your planting design.

Punctuation Correctly placed, an eyecatcher can break the repetition of your plantings, acting as a 'punctuation mark' in the material – but resist the temptation use it too often. Whatever you choose as a punctuation mark needs to be in the same vein as the general planting. A mass of shrub roses with a blue conifer in the midst would not sit well, though substitute that conifer with a smoke bush (*Cotinus* spp.), or a California lilac (*Ceanothus* spp.) and you achieve a far more satisfactory harmony to the planting design.

Layering In practical horticultural terms layering is a cultivation technique. What I am referring to are layers of plant material, perhaps of contrasting plant forms; the Mediterranean landscape, for instance, is naturally layered with vertical cypress, rounded pittosporum and gnarled olive trees. The use of plants with architectural form allows you to layer – it's what you see in elevation – though plenty of ordinary plant material is needed to support a layered effect. You might layer plants successfully when they are used in association with buildings.

Groupings A mass of plants tends to be a finite blob; plant a few of them and you get a staccato effect. Instead, try running together groups of plants to drift one mass into another. Drifting bulbs through small woody material, for instance, is another form of sequential layering. So sequence comes into this concept too.

The meadow technique For the larger garden, what is called the meadow or prairie technique is based upon natural plant association (see page 67). But before we all plump for the easy alternative to regular mowing, I can tell you that those elegant photographs of nodding flower meadows have taken three or four years of hard management – unless you have wildflowers growing naturally, but even then they will usually be of a limited range and they will need mowing, so that your meadow becomes a hayfield. There is far more involved than simply placing grasses at random through perennial material. Which grasses for which soil – in sun or shade? And then there's ground preparation, even the stripping of topsoil – for wild flowers prefer a poor and unamended soil.

Increasingly there is a coming together of the meadow technique with the more traditional use of perennial and woody material. English landscape designer Tom Stuart-Smith is a master of the technique. But space is necessary and the result is often less lawn or grass.

Left The technique of combining ornamental grasses and perennials gives a naturalistic planting of different textures, punctuated by a limited palette of strong colours.

Opposite Tom Stuart-Smith's Telegraph Garden at the Chelsea Flower Show 2006 is a meeting of modernity and romanticism: swathes of cottage planting cut by a formal oak walkway with a wall of pre-rusted steel.

Hard materials

These are the pavings, the wallings or fencings – in general the constructional elements of a garden, which form the basis of your design and its organisation. Very broadly I have suggested that the style of your garden derives from its site, and from the style of house which it surrounds. These two variables must be what help you to decide upon your selection of hard materials.

In an urban situation the house and its construction will be more important than its surround, but as the space gets larger the surrounding landscape has a greater effect on your selection, so that your whole concept integrates better into its site. Of course, you have the option to move from a sophisticated finish near the house and entrance through to a more sympathetic material towards the boundary and external influence, all in one site. It depends upon scale.

I start by looking at local materials, which are the most readily available and are probably the cheapest. And they also look the best. You can see a selection of local materials at your nearest garden centre or builders' merchant.

Natural or man-made?

We have discussed local identity in terms of the character of a site, and it is the materials of which it is made, along with the life it supports (plant as well as human) which creates that identity. Stone reads very clearly in creating identity; mix sandstone in a granite area for instance and it looks wrong. In the US I have found that bluestone belongs very much to the mid-Atlantic region whereas limestone seems better in the Midwest. Softer materials including terracotta are for hotter, more Mediterranean regions (winter frost resistance always being a factor to consider). Where stone is not available you probably have clay, and so bricks come into their own. The same thought process goes into roofing – very much a local identity. Do you use slate, terracotta tile, wood shingle or thatch? And don't discount man-made products, either in reconstituted stone or concrete.

There is also a whole range of products that could be considered handmade from timber. The deck seems currently fashionable in suburban Britain, though it has been used in other parts of the world for ages. The use of timber will depend upon its availability, price, type – and its reaction to the climate. While you may associate South America with adobe buildings, I am working in Patagonia (see page 156) and in this region, in the foothills of the Andes, houses are constructed in timber, therefore it makes sense to extend the feel to surround the house, in conjunction with a local stone.

Another hard surface that you can incorporate is gravel or pebbles. Some gravel comes from quarry chipping; others which are more pebbly and rounded are obtained by dredging. River-washed gravel comes in various sizes and may be used for building – it is also a seaside idiom in some places as well.

So if the choice of hard materials seems wide, what is suitable for your site can be quite restricted. I would urge you to keep your selection simple.

Left Like the plant material you select, the 'hardscape' materials in a garden should be restricted to what is suitable for your site. Pebbles look good in a coastal setting and may suit certain urban contexts where the built environment is dominated by concrete or stone. Gravel is great for creating low-maintenance paths and dry gardens (and it deters the slugs). Wood holds its place, particularly in more rural contexts, for fencing, supports, seating and sometimes as retaining walling if there are different levels. It is readily available and, with the appropriate weather-proofing, can be quite durable. Metal can work surprisingly well – I have used it to construct pergolas, for instance – often where a more delicate feel than stone or timber is required, and the rich patina of aged metal is finding favour with many garden designers.

"Stone reads very clearly in creating identity; mix sandstone in a granite area for instance and it looks wrong."

Time

Time is the fourth dimension in garden design, for it has to do with growth. Your proportions may be excellent when you design a planting layout on paper, but how will it look five or even ten years hence? For how long will the scale of your structure be in keeping with the scale of your planting? If you are working on the grand scale, you need to know how far apart to plant oak trees for instance - for the sake of future generations.

At this stage I think you need to think in terms of a town garden, a larger suburban one and on the country scale. The consideration here is not only the size of the site and the plants you put in it, but also the time span the family (or your client) plans to live there. This latter is probably indefinable for many people, but others can be more definite - until retirement for instance, or while the kids are at the right school.

Outward and upward
The time span for a town garden is, I would suggest, pretty short and in any case you are probably not going to be planting forest trees - I hope. Roots undermining walls come to mind; using up the moisture; too much shade; too many leaves in autumn - these are the issues to be aware of when making your tree choice.

All the same, when planting smaller trees and shrubs, you need to know how far apart to place them and how big they will eventually grow in terms of both height and girth, and over what period of time. True, this sort of detail about perennials at garden centres has become much better over the years but the best source of information comes from a reputable nurseryman's catalogue. Dictionaries are fine, but do not make your selection from a tiny photograph of the flower alone - read the full description, and of course ensure that your choice is commercially available.

In small sites there is always a toss up between planting closely for instant effect, versus more economical planting with a look to the future - spacing the plants at distances apart so that they grow together in five years. The short-term fix means either endless pruning (and where do you put the cuttings?), or thinning out what you have planted altogether.

The classic mistake is to plant a hedge of *Cupressocyparis leylandii* in too small a space, and probably too close together into the bargain. Leylandii

achieve 10 metres in no time at all - and do not stop miraculously. You can take out the top to allow light to your neighbour's windows, but then the hedge bushes out, and the lower growth dies, so that you can see through - so you fence, and so it goes on. Never plant this type of hedge: there are plenty of other hedging plants that are not so rampant.

Much the same can be said for the suburban garden, which might be larger than its town equivalent. Your selection of trees and shrubs might be different - more robust, for instance, but very broadly for the five-year time span - large shrubs are planted at 2 metres apart, and you scale down according to the ultimate breadth of the plant. Inevitably, the planting will look thin for a year or so, but with adequate maintenance things do grow fast. Meanwhile, you introduce what I call the flotsam (see page 113), using climbers or pots sown with annuals: sunflowers, nicotiana, nasturtiums and so on. And of course bulbs for spring too. This approach speeds up the filling process enormously.

Larger gardens will use more robust plants - though the distances at which you plant them may not be much different from a suburban context. On larger sites you may interplant fast-growing deciduous shrubs through slower growing evergreen ones.

If you are a designer or plants-person, remember to keep your proposals for a client comparatively simple, unless the clients know what they are doing; you are not going to be involved in the plant maintenance yourself. Simplicity will be much bolder and stronger than a more involved plan. Remember too that time goes very fast, and plants grow fast as well.

Opposite Faced with a cleared site, it is all too tempting to fill it with plants for instant effect. It pays to resist the short-term fix.

Left I once used paper cut-outs on the ground to demonstrate how a planting scheme fills out a space. It made the point far better than setting out the immature plants still in their pots from the nursery.

Below The mature planting.

3 Context & Technique

The garden designer has, of course, certain presentation techniques, which may relate to the drawing board or to the computer screen, and I have already referred to a design language. Most designers will also employ photography and, I hope, a sketching technique, but none of this is any good without a philosophy and a vision. It is visual experience, based on some early fundamentals, that I would like to explore for universal gardening techniques – very much based upon the Edwardian gardeners' way of doing things. This is the way that still tends to prevail, in Britain at least. And it is to Britain that I wish to refer by way of example. After all, it is the place I know best, and I could explore few other ecosystems in the same detail.

Exploration is the keyword here; for one is trying to distil in gardening terms the work of other and greater explorers in the area. Oliver Rackham, Cambridge botanist and an acknowledged authority on the British countryside, first introduced me to the wider landscape in his *History of the Countryside*. Likewise, the fascinating diaries of the English writer, historian and expert on country houses, James Lees-Milne, are an insight into how the old social system worked and made me realise how much landowners had controlled our landscapes.

At the other end of the spectrum, Flora Thompson's book *Lark Rise to Candleford* showed how life was lived upon the land. Gertrude Jekyll was wonderfully perceptive in her writings on cottage gardens in *Wood and Garden* which she then interpreted on a grander garden scale.

Left The gardens of great houses such as Chatsworth, one of the treasures of the English Midlands, have been developed since the 17th century (in front of the house) with the 18th-century landscaped park beyond and the 19th-century cascade and fountain in the foreground. Twentieth-century touches were more economic, but continued the trend.

Opposite Peter Randall-Page's sculptures make the link between art and the environment.

"Contemplate how, when asked as a designer, you can contribute to this ongoing identification process that combats the threat of uniformity."

Coming more up to date the writing in America of Ian McHarg (a Scotsman), founder of the Department of Landscape Architecture at the University of Pennsylvania, was a huge step forward. In his book, *Design with Nature* (1969), he pioneered the idea of ecological planning. The German Karl Forster distilled these ideas into horticultural terms.

In the present century the work of James Hitchmough and Nigel Dunnett at Sheffield University has been enormously stimulating, and with it a book by Sue Clifford and Angela King, *England in Particular: A Celebration of the Commonplace, the Local, the Vernacular and the Distinctive*. It surveys our impact on, and our relationship with, the English landscape. Very little to do with gardening you might say, but everything to do with thinking about where and how we live. Surely this leads us, as designers and as individuals, to contemplate how we contribute to this on-going identification process, and impels us to combat the threat of uniformity that is imposed upon us by corporate culture?

Sculptors and painters help too, for theirs is now a school that evolves its art out of its landscape and this I really enjoy.

Geographical regions are not defined by land mass, rather by land type. And physical features such as rivers and mountains define areas more obviously than any man-made boundaries.

Much of the feel is to do with topography, the relief or lie of the land, which determines whether it is flat and open like fenland, steppe or prairie, or rolling like downland or wolds, fringe moorland or mountain slope.

These changing landscapes alter in great measure according to the diversity of types and ages of rock that form the backbone of the ground beneath them, which in Britain was further moulded by glacial and post-glacial action.

Over the millennia, the effect of rain, wind, ice and sun has eroded the land surfaces into finer rock particles which, combined with water and organic matter, have produced our soils. The British Isles contain many different soil types and the nature of these soils characterises the various regions and, in turn, the vegetation growing upon them. These can broadly be categorised as heath and moorland, open grassland including downland, wetland, coastland and mountains.

But the original flora over by far the greater area of the country – as indeed across much of the northern hemisphere – was woodland. As the ice receded, cold-tolerant dwarf willow, juniper and small birches came first. Then, as the birches grew larger, pinewoods developed in the southeast of the country.

From forest to field

With the gradual warming of the climate, pines and birches spread north, with rowan, aspen, then hazel, alder and lime filling in behind. By the time rising sea levels separated England from France and Holland, it had great forests of lime, oak, elm and alder with, later, beech, ash and maple. Forests expanded to cover at least two-thirds of the country, though as man changed

Above left The more extreme the climate the more specific the plants. In the foothills of the Rockies, Colorado, cold and snow inhibit many trees, though spruce (*Picea* spp.) and white pine are common.

Left A Mediterranean plant association of drought-tolerant cypress with Aleppo pine (*Pinus halepensis*) with a characteristic underplanting of myrtle (*Myrtus communis*) and rock rose (*Cistus* spp).

from hunter-gatherer to crop-grower and herdsman, he started to encroach into these ancient wild woods by burning, clearing then ploughing. Wetlands too were exploited for reed, sedge and peat.

As Saxon culture emerged after Roman, groups of thatch and timber huts clustered together into hamlets, and a farming culture started to develop on an infield and outfield system. The infield was worked together, intensely cultivated and manned; the rougher outfields beyond were grazed. Hazel was the universal fuel, with younger wood woven into wattle work and faggots for general domestic use. Ash was in demand for gates and weapons, beech for furniture, maple for making bowls, and alder or ash for hop poles.

This continuing development of the land continued until the Black Death of the 14th century, during which time whole villages were wiped out, fields were abandoned and much cultivated land reverted to woodland.

From common land to enclosure

Those who survived the Plague, however, could command huge wages owing to manpower shortage and gradually, with savings, buy farmland, which the new owner might even enclose with walls or hedges. And so communities expanded again, some of them into market towns.

More and more open land was enclosed as farmers sought to improve their stock. In the 18th and 19th centuries Enclosure Acts affected at least 3,000 English parishes and by 1860 nearly half of Britain was enclosed as private property. The impact on the landscape during this period showed as a rectilinear field pattern on much of the English Midlands, defined by straight walls, hedges and fences.

The ancient practice of coppicing woodland declined from the 18th century as alternative fuels became available. Many woods were cleared and replanted as commercial forest or cleared altogether for farming.

The current picture is of a patchwork of woodland of varying ages and open ground, which might be arable (though the field sizes are far larger, with many hedgerows removed to facilitate the movement of cumbersome farm machinery), common ground, downland or pasture – heath or moorland, even wetland – and all surrounded by our coastal landscapes.

So why recount the historical changes to the landscape of Britain? The reason is this: each environment will have its own typical vegetation, totally out of scale with the average garden but nevertheless part of the jigsaw. If you understand the basis of the overall picture your piece of jigsaw will fit in far more comfortably.

Right Key trees identify different parts of the world. From left to right: the Australian eucalyptus, the European oak, the palm of the Tropics and *Araucaria* or the monkey puzzle of central South America.

Analysis: Soil

Soil is the basic medium in which everything grows. Topsoil (for that is what we are in fact talking about) in certain parts of the world can be deep and rich in organic matter where it was once woodland or jungle, built up over generations by falling leaves and, when on contoured ground, held firmly in place by the roots of the trees which feed on it so constantly. Clear-felling for a quick catch crop allows in heavy monsoon rain, which washes that precious soil downstream.

In other parts of the world topsoil is so thin and scarce, it barely supports any life at all. No life, no food for cattle or for the people who herd them. Where plant material is scarce, the population turns to sheep and goats, whose close nibbling of whatever is available only compounds the world's food problem. No more 'Buy a goat for Christmas', please!

The land on a world scale

To write about soil as a garden commodity - and whether our bit of it is acid or alkaline - becomes almost frivolous in these global terms. We are so fortunate in a temperate climate to have any at all.

The stewardship of the land and its soils has to become a major concern. With the decline in arable and mixed farming our landscapes, once fashioned by being worked in different ways, are increasingly being allowed to stand idle and revert to scrub and then woodland - or to become a golf course or a leisure park. Much is being flooded on the one hand to provide water in an increasingly globally warmed world, while on the other famous wetlands (for annual bird migration) are being drained to provide housing. The fact that structures are going up on a floodplain is being totally ignored: when it does rain, the water floods in all too easily.

This makes a very broad view of our world landscapes and the need for a new thinking far more inclusive than in mere garden terms.

Local awareness

With the recent increased interest in ecology and plant association, perversely our concerns have also to be scaled right down to our own particular piece of ground and, as gardeners, we need to be aware of what grows naturally there.

With a little knowledge of your local environment, it is possible to roughly gauge the chemical make-up of your soil type, without needing to be specific on pH type, remembering that very broadly most plants will grow in most places. It is extremes of acidity, alkalinity and/or wetness that makes things difficult.

In general terms, much of what is now heath and moorland in north temperate latitudes was once pine, birch and oak forest. Acid-loving plants are mostly from woodland areas and prefer cool, more or less shady environments and soil that is humus rich, moist but not waterlogged. With the loss of native woodland cover through cultivation, the soils were depleted of much of their fertility. In the lowlands of Britain, for example, where the bedrock is acidic, poor soils supporting only heath (heather, ling, gorse, bracken and fine acid-loving grasses) developed; on higher ground, especially where rainfall was high and the bedrock impervious, infertile soils became peat-based moorland.

Once the native tree cover was cleared from more fertile, alkaline (lime-rich) soils, grassland developed, but it could only be prevented from reverting to scrub by being constantly grazed or mown. Downland pasture on chalk or limestone is maintained by grazing animals such as sheep (and rabbits). If the grass is undisturbed by ploughing, it may support a rich display of wild flowers. The pervious nature of the bedrock, though, means that water retention is a problem of alkaline soils.

Swamps, bogs, marshes and fens develop wherever water collects, either naturally or through the actions of humans. The land may be permanently or seasonally waterlogged and typically supports grasses, sedges, rushes, irises and ferns in lo-lying areas. If the land starts to dry out, or is drained for agriculture, the natural vegetation changes to support willow, birch and alder.

By observing nature, you can select garden plants, not necessarily native but sometimes a less rampant form, that will not only thrive in the soil type but also fit the locality.

Clockwise, from top left Upland locations with thin, fast-draining soils may show the vestiges of former pine forest; deciduous woodland on more favoured, wetter lowland sites will have more acid, humus-rich soils; semi-tropical forests have more evergreen plants, meaning most nutrients remain in the vegetation itself, not the soil; in waterlogged conditions, peatbogs and swamps develop.

Analysis: Natural history

Britain's native planting is incredibly rich in its variety. Prime time for flowers is May or June when even roadside verges are quite glorious in their variety. Autumn brings colour in turning foliage and plains of purple heather in the north. Winter, though in parts all black and brown, can, I think, be wonderful too, depending on the location. Later winter and early spring have interesting detail – early primroses, native hellebores, catkins and the like, giving way to drifts of bluebells beneath unfurling leaves.

The painter captures these seasonal moments – the poet too. But take a look at the pages of a nurseryman's catalogue and note they are worlds apart. Why is this? With our increasing awareness and sensitivity to environmental issues surely some essence of what grows best in our countryside should be present in those multi-coloured pages. Why do we so hanker after the bizarre, and why do new garden designers pull away from the traditional materials of landscape to introduce alien inorganic substances?

It is, I suppose, that we want to be different, and do our own thing, and once the frenzy is upon us there is no stopping. But take a look at any stretch of seemingly natural landscape and where an alien conifer pops up you know that someone has built a 19th- or 20th-century garden there. Not to mention 20th-century forestry in parts and its unsympathetic blanket planting, now amended I believe. What I am asking is why, if we love our countryside, do we seek to plant in our gardens almost entirely alien subjects? It might be to do with scale, it might be to do with the invasive quality of some of our natives, it is probably to do with hankering after what we saw during a summer holiday, with wanting longer periods of sustainable colour and hence interest.

What we can do is to learn from nature and her plant associations. And this gets you thinking environmentally. To consider what is damp and what is dry; to think out what is in the sun and what is in shade. To consider the consistency of a soil and whether its water-holding capacity can be improved by the addition of organic matter. Feed the soil for vegetable growing by all means, but improve the soil to hold water in other areas.

In each of these and dozens of other habitats you will find keynote plants, and accompanying drifts – the range is often quite limited over a small area (and admittedly lacks that long season colour interest), but do we want chrysanthemums all year round and isn't the static Florida vegetation boring?

"The changing of the seasons has always been of vital importance for humans."

Seasonal change

The changing of the seasons has always been of vital importance for humans, marked by pagan festivals right from the earliest of our ancestors. We tend to shudder at the winter season, but it has its moments, especially when frosted. Spare a thought for the seasonal cycle – and the wildlife that depends upon it – when the next bright catalogue plops through your letterbox. It is not a rustic environment one seeks, just a truthful ongoing, natural annual cycle of vegetation and events which complements both natural planting about it, and the resonances of what happened before.

So, wherever you live, try to understand that the area originally had a particular type of vegetation that was specific to that altitude, topography, weather and soil. Its plant material developed over the millennia as humans adapted and refined the land and landscape to their pastoral lifestyle so that there was a harmony between nature and humans. The harmony was further strengthened by particular vernacular idioms – that is being part of and built using only the material available locally.

Opposite English natural vegetation is comparatively benign. Much of it crept into the cottage garden palette of plant material. Here you see foxgloves (*Digitalis purpurea*) with Shasta daisies (*Leucanthemum superbum*), now hybridised.

Analysis: Local traditions

As soon as building starts, a vernacular develops as well, for early builders could only afford to use local materials, and in Europe this continued right into the industrialisation and emergent mass-market culture of the 19th century. If you had wealth, however, and with it education, you displayed that by importing alien building materials and building in foreign styles, all decorated with imported furniture and art works, which you had collected on your travels.

Parallel with this form of gracious living, however, and much more in evidence in the countryside, was the development of built communities constructed in the local idiom and using whatever timber, brick or stone was available. The people who lived in these farms and cottages managed the land, according to its type – grassland, woodland, wetland, or moorland –

so that there was a natural cycle of rock, soil, growth, and land management. This was an interdependent culture, trademarked (for want of a better expression) by its own vernacular.

Identifying a vernacular style

Vernacular idioms and hence building materials can be traced not county by county or state by state, but region by region. In Britain you find Scottish granite, border slate, Midland and Northeast stone, clay from the clay belts of the midlands, Norfolk and Suffolk, chalk of the Chilterns and South Downs, and the West Country sandstone and granite in Cornwall. The vernacular extends to walls, barns, fences, and field shapes, each a celebration of a type of farming once practised in the area, one that also has its own associated plants and wildlife.

So cultural landscapes have developed from local nature and day-to-day human history. As garden and landscape designers, we must be aware not only of what has gone before, but what that same land reveals now. For while houses and lifestyles might have changed, the underlying parent rock, stone, and earth and what grows upon them has not. I believe that we should look and listen to a site to hear its stories, and at least try to establish some dialogue with it. Taken collectively, our gardens represent a considerable area of the landscape. We should do well to remember that our impact upon it may last longer than our tenure of that place. Covering your piece of earth with synthetic decking, building a swimming pool filled with chemicals or a fibreglass waterfall, or importing a tree fern from the other side of the world seems, to me, nothing short of tragic.

Below, left to right Each country displays similar, though different, regional identities. Contrasting the English cottage example here are timber in the American Midwest, bamboo, as used everywhere in the Far East, and adobe – a major component of desert landscapes.

Designing: Photography

000365.jpg

Above The image from a digital camera is an instant record of a site, and can be imported into a CAD program. (**Insert**) The slide gives a more professional result. Both are important tools for the designer.

I am the last person to go into the technology of photography. My faithful old Pentax has served me well, but I have noticed that it is not the quality of the camera which makes a good photograph, it is whether you can compose a picture or not. Remember, we are essentially trying to compose pictures when we design a garden.

For years I have taken slides for a number of reasons. Firstly, of course, I use photographs to record a site so that I can revisit it at my drawing board. The shots from your camera can tell you whether doors open in or out, whether they are sliding or French doors, whether there is brick or stone, as well as capturing the boundaries and the plant profile both inside and outside the site. In addition, the photographs will record things you have on your checklist but which, in the heat of the moment, you forgot to note down. Sometimes if the client won't leave you alone on site, you may have to insist on or rather ask for some thinking time so that you don't miss the all-important details.

But the days of slides seem numbered, and photographic prints, while better than nothing, are not the same. Now I carry a digital camera with me, so that I find I visit a site with two cameras, just in case. While the digital camera is much more immediate, and I can do my own printing, it is important to store and archive all the images you take for easy access. Although, it has to be said that I'm still not entirely computer-proficient – old dog, new tricks sort of thing!

However, I do use digital imagery all the time these days as the basis for the sketches which accompany my outline proposals to the client. By craftily combining the photographs and the drawings, you can give your clients a very good idea of your intentions, as they can recognise their site in your image, and 'read' your proposals much more easily. Quite often, you may find that, having slaved over a drawing, a client cannot readily visualise it. This does not negate the necessity for a drawing, though, as it still forces you, the designer, to work to scale and to be realistic in your concept. So, in order to supplement the drawing I take my scissors to the digital prints, cut out what I am about to alter and draw in (taking my perspective from the photograph) what I subsequently propose. It may seem low-tech but I find it works as an accompaniment to my initial proposal to the client.

With digital images you can make up a collage – and these are the sort of prints that you can cut out and then proceed to combine them with your own proposals on overlay (see pages 72–3).

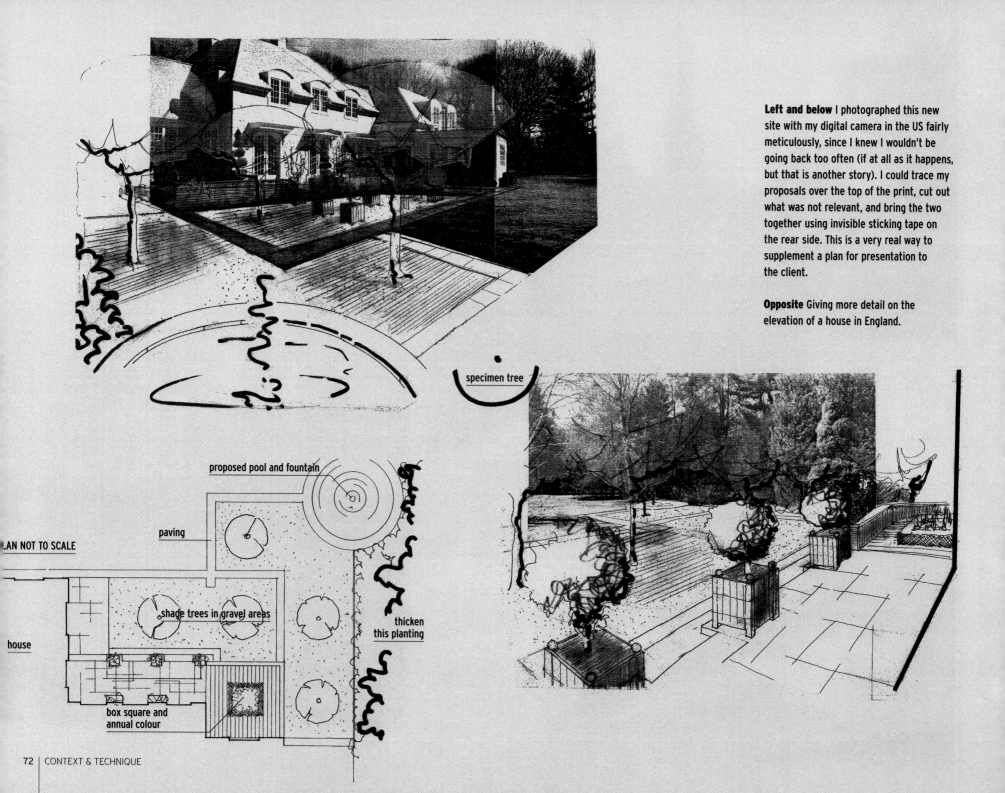

Left and below I photographed this new site with my digital camera in the US fairly meticulously, since I knew I wouldn't be going back too often (if at all as it happens, but that is another story). I could trace my proposals over the top of the print, cut out what was not relevant, and bring the two together using invisible sticking tape on the rear side. This is a very real way to supplement a plan for presentation to the client.

Opposite Giving more detail on the elevation of a house in England.

specimen tree

proposed pool and fountain

paving

PLAN NOT TO SCALE

house

shade trees in gravel areas

thicken this planting

box square and annual colour

Drafting: Measuring the site

There is little point in developing a design of a site, unless it is subsequently drawn to scale. You can play about with ideas not to scale but when it comes to the presentation crunch I think that the layout must accurately fit the site.

Always ask your clients whether they have anything already on a surveyed plan of their site. There are often mumblings about "There was a bit of something on the plan for the extension", and sure enough the plan of the entire house is there - with an outline of the site at least - which is a great help.

Where no survey is available, for your first presentation, provided the site is not too large, too irregular or too wooded, take the measurements yourself. If it is a really difficult site I suggest you explain to the clients that you need to have a survey professionally drawn up (and will they arrange it, or will you?). The garden designer's life becomes much easier with a survey. That said, you'll need to check it: surveyors tend not to be botanists, and their plant identification can sometimes be plain wrong.

On smaller sites you can measure up with tapes and skewers or use the newer laser technique to record the dimensions. Either way, you will need to get those measurements down on a drawing. When you are working outside, paper on a clipboard and a hardish pencil - 2H perhaps - are essential (if you use a pen or ballpoint and it rains, everything runs on the page). First establish roughly the house position on site, as you see it. Then put in the doors and windows, again as you see them. From a corner of the house take running measurements along all the relevant faces of it - noting doors and windows. Fix your tape with a skewer.

Once you have positioned the features of the house - take offsets from it - either at right angles to it, or triangulate, to establish the boundaries of the site. Then, by the same method, infill the details - existing trees, any other buildings, existing pathways and so on. Even if you are going to eliminate some of that details, get it down initially on your survey.

Next photograph your house elevations and as much of the site details as possible. Accompany your survey and photos with notes to yourself of the views, of the prevailing wind, what you intend to keep and what will go.

You will probably not need a detailed survey until your client has accepted your initial ideas and sketches, but even these elements should have some measure of accuracy to them. They are vital to the following stages.

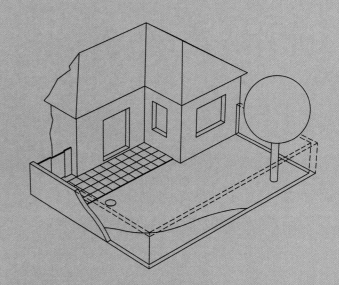

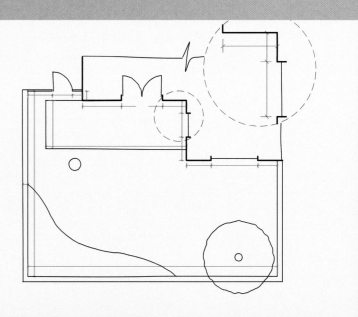

1 Taking the measurements
Draw and measure up the house and all its features - doors and windows in particular. If the site is obviously regular put in boundaries and feature trees.

Right Peter, my assistant, working along the façade of a building noting the running dimensions of its features. It is best to work solo: talking to someone makes it hard to take on board the details of the site.

Centre and far right Taking an offset to a feature tree from the house and then using a second tape from another fixed position to triangulate and fix the tree's position accurately on site.

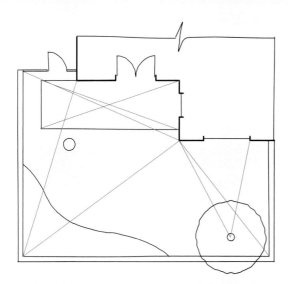

2 Calculating positions

To accurately fix features in the garden you need to triangulate measurements from already determined points.

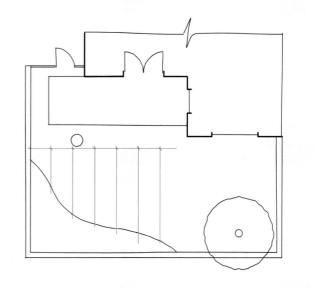

3 Surveying a curve

To fix a curving or, in this case, a wiggly line, take regular offsets at 90° to a known horizontal. The terrace line could also have been used.

Drafting: Drawing skills

Despite the more high-tech alternatives, I think that drafting skills are still very important for the garden and landscape designer. Initially drawing out on page allows one to explore one's ideas. Now I am well aware of the accusation of being Luddite in my scepticism of CAD drawings, but that is not the whole truth: many final renderings by CAD are superb (see pages 80-1), and I find it an excellent medium for surveys, drainage plans, constructional details and the more mechanical side of drafting. But for conceptual drawings and plantings, and indeed small projects, I still prefer drafting on a board. I also think that clients feel that they have got something prepared especially for them, rather than churned out by a program.

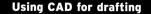

Using CAD for drafting

CAD is precise and requires accurate sketches or measurements for input. There are several ways to get your design into CAD but they all work from a basic premise:

- You can import a scanned image of an accurate pencil sketch and trace using the CAD drawing tools.

- Or, input a scanned image of a site plan or survey and trace it with CAD tools.

- Or, import an AutoCAD file and use it as a base plan.

- Or, finally, manually input site measurements using the CAD tools.

If you prefer to develop design ideas through hand sketches you can draw or trace the base plan on CAD and print it out to scale on top of the printed copy. Once the ideas are fixed they can be scanned and traced onto the CAD base plan.

Opposite Some of the tools of a CAD program. With a click of the mouse the symbol for a particular planting can be selected or an area infilled with a type of hatching to show the proposed material. These programs speed up the drafting process, but there is still a place for working on a board.

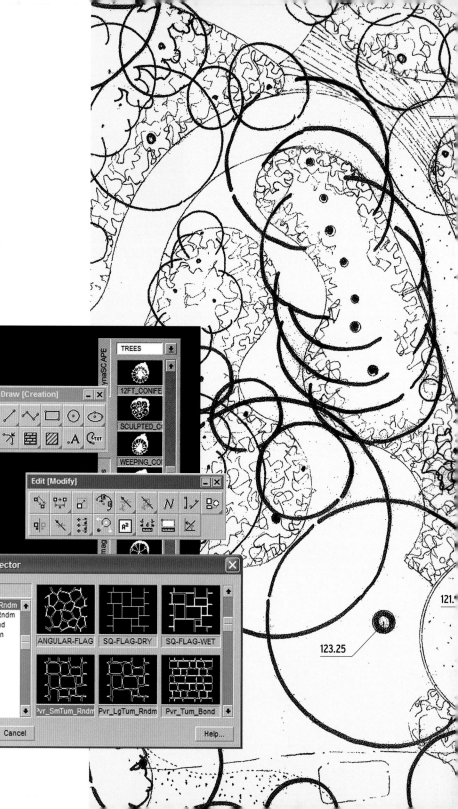

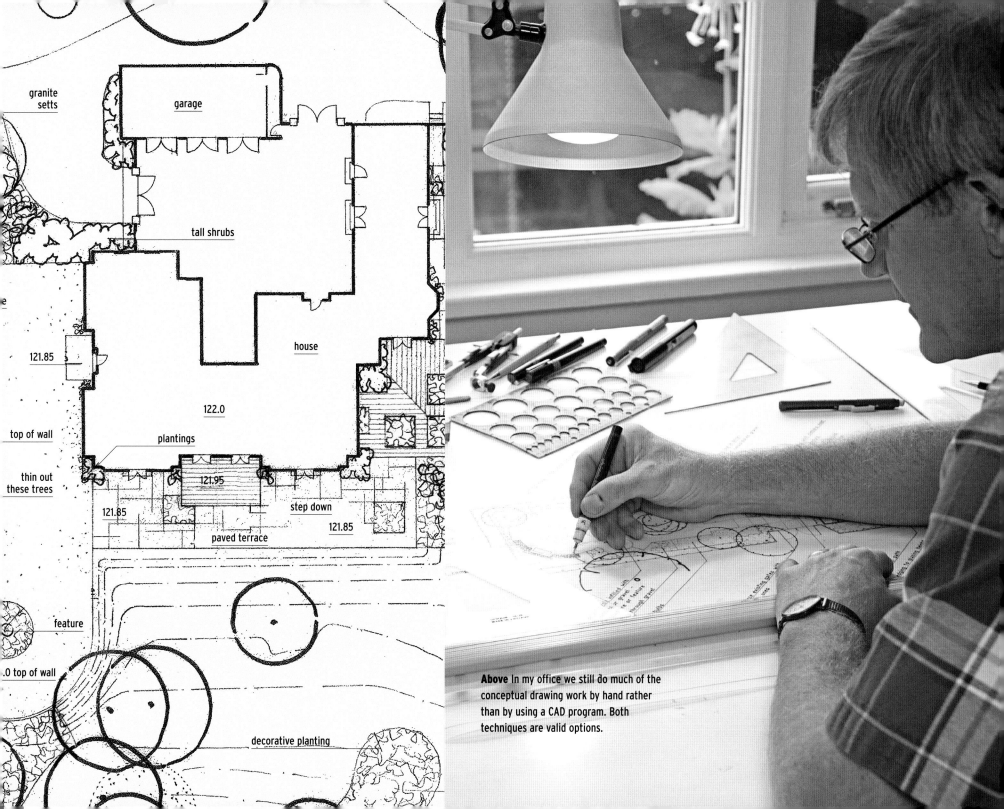

granite
setts

garage

tall shrubs

house

121.85

top of wall

122.0

thin out
these trees

plantings

121.95

121.85

step down

121.85

paved terrace

feature

.0 top of wall

decorative planting

Above In my office we still do much of the
conceptual drawing work by hand rather
than by using a CAD program. Both
techniques are valid options.

Drafting: Drawing to scale

In preparing your plan, there is no point in not drawing to scale, and the scale you select will depend upon the content of the plan. It is helpful if the plan fits upon your sheet of tracing paper – that goes without saying – and this in turn depends upon the size of your site!

Ideally you want a good presentation with everything coming together – so you select your scale accordingly. It is a pretty big site that needs to be presented at scale 1:500; curiously the scale down from that used in landscape work is scale 1:200, then 1:100 (or 1/8″ – 1′0″ for the US). The scale mostly used for initial presentations is probably 1:100. Half that scale 1:50

(1/16″ – 1′0″) is the scale to use for construction or for a detailed planting with small perennials.

Scaling your drawings up or down is labour-intensive. Have it done mechanically at your local print shop and while you are there check on all the other procedures that are now possible, such as reversing a drawing white out of black, laminating it, and scanning it to e-mail to a client abroad. (Incidentally I have printed A2 size sheets of trace, so everything is standardised. One-off sizes are difficult to start with.) If you are working with CAD (see pages 80-1) there is, of course, absolutely no problem with either enlarging or reducing a drawing.

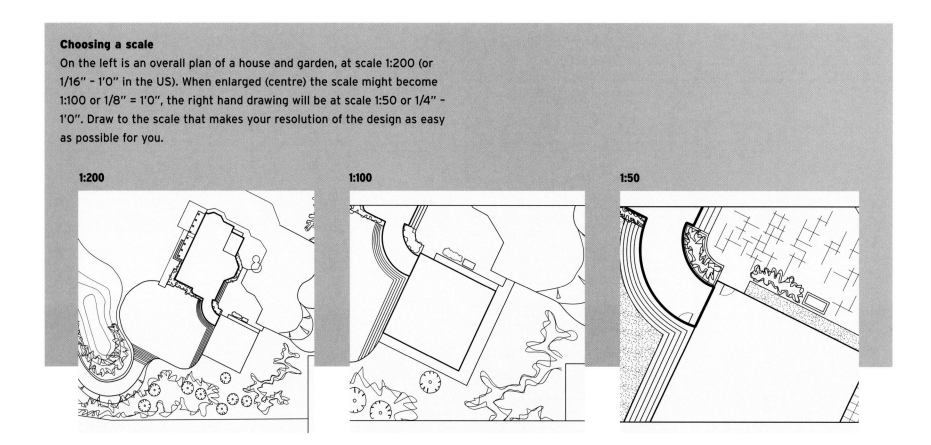

Choosing a scale
On the left is an overall plan of a house and garden, at scale 1:200 (or 1/16″ – 1′0″ in the US). When enlarged (centre) the scale might become 1:100 or 1/8″ = 1′0″, the right hand drawing will be at scale 1:50 or 1/4″ – 1′0″. Draw to the scale that makes your resolution of the design as easy as possible for you.

1:200

1:100

1:50

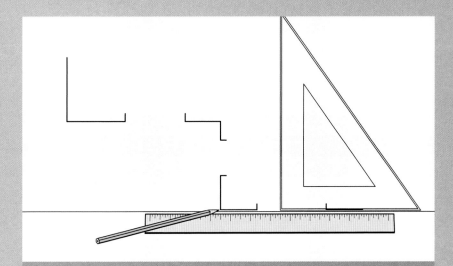

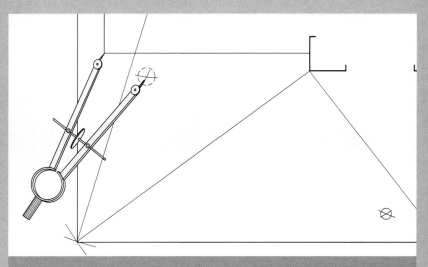

1 **Drawing up the outlines**
The instructions here are very basic. Use a hard pencil (2H), kept sharp. That yellow measure is a scale, not a ruler. You should use two triangles with a T square on your drawing board.

2 **Drawing up the outlines**
Be precise and accurate at all times.

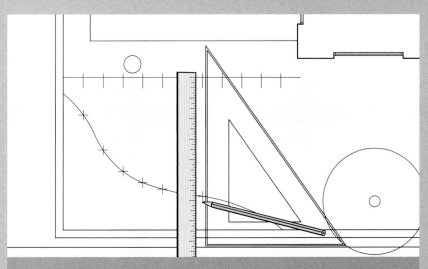

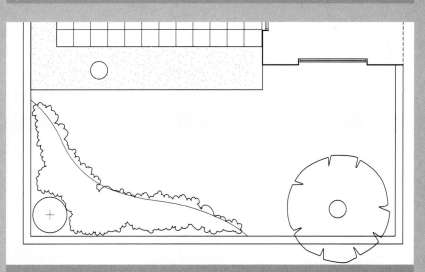

3 **Drawing up a garden curve**
Take offsets at regular intervals from either a line parallel to the house or from the house itself, and then join them up to define the line.

4 **Adding detail**
Give body to your survey by defining surfaces, plant material, tree overhangs and their girth.

Drafting: Using CAD

CAD has simplified the whole procedure of preparing working drawings. You need only to create one master plan and use the 'layers' function of CAD, turning the various layers on and off to show the elements required for the working drawing you wish to produce or print for a client. You can present a planting plan, a dimension plan, a 'hardscape' or material construction plan, an irrigation plan, a lighting plan, etc. The huge advantage of CAD is that there is no need to have to re-draw the plan to achieve these multiple options.

Some programs include an extensive set of pre-drawn landscape symbols to represent all elements of the design. Once again, this saves you, the garden designer, time by not having to draw each elements every time you want to show one, particularly if the symbol contains a lot of detail such as brickwork or a type of paving. The symbols are all drawn to a proper scale, use the correct line weights, and have a style that renders a hand-drawn (or nearly so!) appearance.

Photographs of plants or any other landscape element can be easily pasted, sized and moved around on the CAD drawing itself. The drawings can then be printed with leader lines and colored images for a highly visual presentation which is very immediate for the client.

The ease of making revisions is where CAD programs can really shine. Unlike pencil or ink drawings, the CAD version can easily be changed without erasing, smudging or redrawing. The CAD editing tool can erase, move, rescale, rotate and duplicate objects quickly and easily. This is where there are huge time savings to be made, which can become especially important if the client is fussy or the project costs are getting too high.

The best CAD programs include a link to an on-line Plant Encyclopedia, allowing the designer ready access to images and cultural information about plants. The plant pictures can be sourced via a search tool or automatically matched through the plant label and then placed anywhere on the CAD design. Once a plan is labelled, plant lists can be generated from that plan at speed. As a bonus, plant care packages can be automatically generated from the plant list where it is matched up with images and care instructions from the on-line Plant Encyclopedia.

Left The CAD worker can combine the advantages of an on-line Plant Encyclopedia and a set of pre-drawn symbols to prepare a working plan at speed. Adjustments can be made without any need for re-drawing.

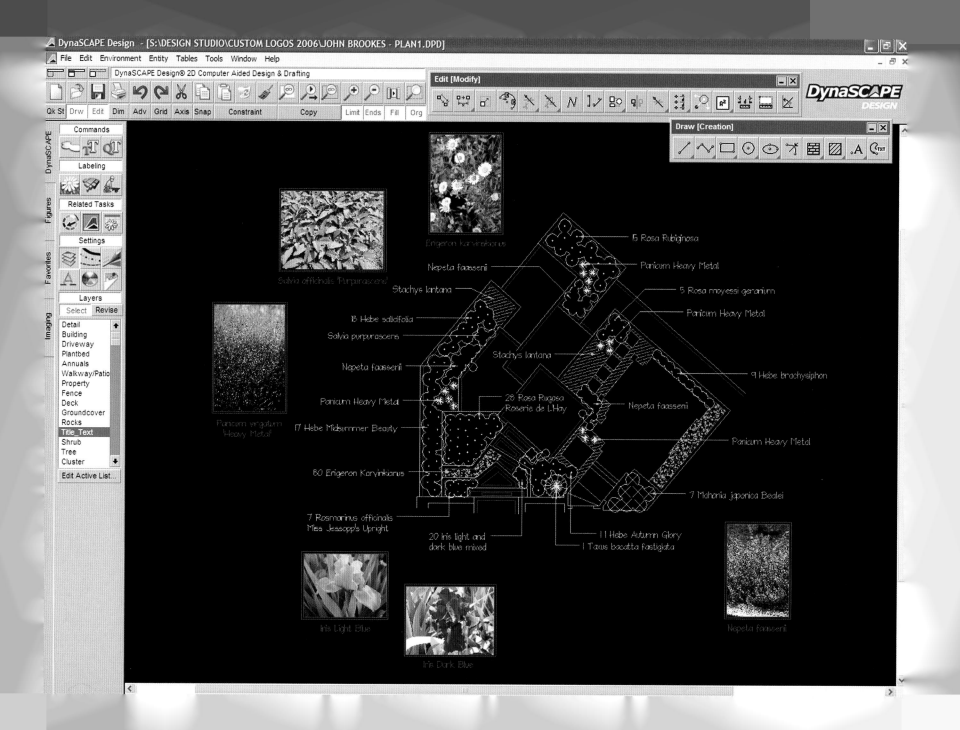

Drafting: Working with the proportions of your site

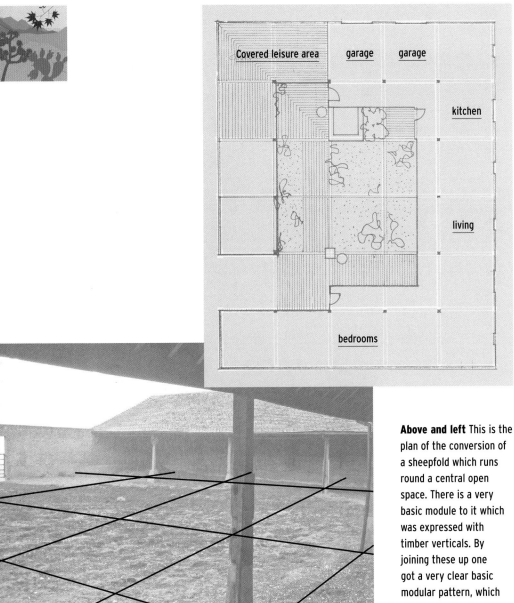

Covered leisure area   garage   garage

kitchen

living

bedrooms

Above and left This is the plan of the conversion of a sheepfold which runs round a central open space. There is a very basic module to it which was expressed with timber verticals. By joining these up one got a very clear basic modular pattern, which will be paved with areas of planted gravel between.

When I was first learning about garden design, I do not seem to remember anyone telling me how to get going, and yet this is the hardest part when you are new to trying to visualise a design concept.

As a teacher I wanted to find a way to get students to loosen up, to forget plants and gardens, and to think instead about pattern (which is what a garden plan is). So we looked at the work of abstract painters, field patterns, buildings, to see how, in plan form, you can designate all sorts of rooms in all sorts of sizes, but they usually have a sequence and logic to their placement. Furthermore they have proportionate relationships to each other – all related to the scale of the human being. Many architectural plans are drawn up either by hand or digitally on a basic grid – which looks like a piece of graph paper. The square sizes are decided by the architect, not the printer, often to suit the size in which basic building components are made.

The basic module

We started by looking at basic house plans to discover the module size on which they were built. I then figured that if you begin to evolve a garden plan on the same module size as the house, you start to get a design relationship between the inside and outside of the house. When concentrating on the outside, however, you can halve or quarter the module if you are drawing a detailed paving pattern, for instance, or double or treble it (it is still proportional) if you are designing a bold, sweeping landscape.

I would then ask the students to transpose their patterns into this standard module size, or grid, so that they too were proportional to the building. Using landscape colours of brown, green and blue, we then started to turn the modular pattern into a garden plan – colouring areas appropriate to their position and relationship to the house. Free shapes do not fit into a grid and they had to be turned into a geometry with circles, segments of circles, interlocking circles and so on. So eventually we were producing structured designs which had a logic to them. Next, we would add orientation into the sequence (north, south, east or west) and then an imaginary brief from the client – a terrace in shade, a pool, a herb garden, compost bins and so on – which we would draw loosely in pencil first, inking them in later on.

Left The module can clearly be seen relating to the elevation of this Mediterranean villa. To detail areas close to the house, the grid could be halved again.

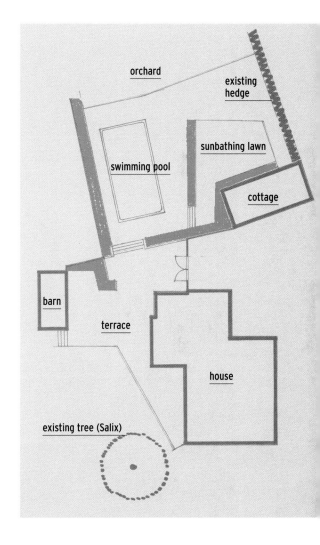

Right The layout of older properties often does not lend itself to the modular approach when I would start to take lines off existing buildings to divide up the spaces. So, in this plan, the terrace between house and barn becomes one room, the swimming pool surround another, with the cottage and sunbathing lawn as well. Spaces may be further defined with different surfacing materials.

The value of the grid system

I still think this grid system works and it certainly gets the fledgling garden designer started. I refer back to it from time to time, but my answer to the inevitable question "Do you still use the grid?", is probably "Not too often", but in fact I do still use it, albeit less rigidly.

I always explain to students that the grid is not a straitjacket, just a way of getting you to think proportionately – but it is a good discipline, and I can tell by looking at students' work if they have understood this basic underlying necessity for a proportionate logic to their designs. Another way to achieve a similar result is to use the lines of the house plan and extend them into the garden, possibly taking the line of a building extension or a bay window to start to form the module – a wide sliding door makes an obvious feature on which to base your grid, since any terrace subsequently built will need to reflect this subdivision. The designer always needs to keep the basic proportions in mind, however, since it is all too easy to end up with a sort of tartan pattern.

There is a school of thought in landscape architecture that you should let 'logic lines' develop across a site – these fall where people naturally want to walk. This can work on a domestic level, but the logic lines tend to be given to paths or pavings on an existing site which the client does not want to move. Your grid, therefore will somehow need to recognise these too. (You will see much of this theory of using existing levels and pavings in the site I analyse on pages 92-7.)

"I wanted to find a way to get students to loosen up, to forget plants and gardens and just to think about pattern."

4 The Design Process

Now I have built up a skeleton of garden and landscape language based upon a philosophy, and this section summarises the typical process in a design consultation, from an initial meeting with the client, through the presentation of design proposals, to the planning of structures and the layout of planting.

Initial client contact

Clients often contact me by phone, so I arrange to go and see their site on a particular day. I confirm this in writing, setting out my working conditions and fees. I charge for an initial site visit per hour, along with my expenses, and I expect a written acceptance of the fee. I ask the prospective clients to think about and agree on what it is that they actually want. I also ask, just in case, whether the clients have a survey of their site, which is always enormously helpful.

All this presupposes that the clients want an outline plan to be drawn up for the development of their garden, rather than just an on-site consultation. I would normally discuss their expectations and requirements of the visit on the phone. Remember that your new clients often have no idea how a garden designer works and you will need to spell this out to them quite clearly, giving all the options on job procedure.

Job procedure options

The options for a job might be one of the following:

• An on-site consultation alone, at an agreed hourly rate.

• An on-site consultation, followed by drawing up an outline or master plan with no details, at an agreed price.

• An on-site consultation, followed by drawing up an outline or master

plan. After approval of the master plan you may be asked to provide further details of construction – such as steps, low walls, water features, pergola structures and so on – in order that the client can build the job or can invite tenders (or prices) from contractors. For this the clients will need an itemised specification (that is, a step-by-step description of the work). You may then be asked for a planting plan, at an agreed price – your clients might want to do their own work with your input. Decide on this and agree a sum for your drawings.

Alternatively, the client may want you to supervise the construction work – the hard landscape – as well as the ground preparation and planting, known as the soft landscape work. In this case, you would charge on a percentage rate of the value of the contract. These rates are fixed for garden designers by their relevant organisation.

There are, of course, many other permutations. For instance, you may wish to supply the plants yourself. In each case, it is essential that your clients agree to the rates or fees in writing, so that you do not have to haggle at the end of the job – or whenever it finishes for you.

For my work abroad, after the initial visit and then producing a master plan, the clients get a bill. I hope to get another visit before detailing the plan. Thereafter I bill according to when I am in their area to make a site visit, as I try to cut down on individual flights.

So now you roll up to the site.

Opposite The generous timber-built loggia sits easily with the swimming pool terrace in a sub-tropical garden.

The visit

My antenna come out as I approach a new site, usually by car. From the natural vegetation or what is growing in gardens nearby I get a feel for the place.

I often go to meet new clients knowing very little about them, although they might have told me about their garden problem I am there to solve. But the clients themselves are as important as the site. The house, its style and period, and its materials you can see, but the clients are something else again. If you are not invited into the house, you will need to find a way to have a look. If the house is new and empty, or not even built, you can make broad suggestions, but you will not be able to go into detail. Ideally, a chat with your clients over a cup of tea or coffee will help you to get a feel for the house and your clients and, dare I say, work out who makes the decisions as well, or who has an idea of what to expect.

Initial reaction

I personally tend to shoot my mouth off, I think, but the clients are paying for my ideas, so I say exactly what occurs to me as we eventually look at the site, and I mumble something about thinking aloud. In this way, you usually get a reaction, and you can start a constructive conversation about what the clients want and what they do not want (and remember that checklist - see pages 26-7). If you can sketch or draw a sketch plan of your ideas as you go around, so much the better. With luck, you will enthuse the clients enough that they ask you straight away to prepare an outline or master plan. I have some associates who do not charge for this visit, and don't give anything away; and they subsequently write in with their ideas. I could not do that. I get excited about a new site and, I like to think, convey some of that enthusiasm to my client. It probably puts off some clients, too! Your bedside manner is very important at this stage.

Left There is much you can pick up about a place, simply by noticing what is growing naturally in hedgerows and on verges. It is worth taking photographs of the approach to a new site as well.

"I get excited about a new site, and, I like to think, convey some of that enthusiasm to my client."

Above Record the things that make an impression on you, the designer, as you approach a site - a view beyond the garden itself, a particularly sun-filled corner, or an attractive tree or other feature.

Getting the facts down

If it is just a small garden, I would measure up the site there and then, with the clients' agreement, but if it is more complicated - with varying levels, for instance - I ask my clients whether I can arrange to have a proper survey completed after generating an estimate for the work. This is assuming that they don't give you a drawing of the site. However, you might not need levels at this early stage - for whether there are eight or ten steps does not really matter - but you do need to have site measurements, house measurements and know the position and nature of any existing vegetation and trees. (Surveyors are not plantspeople so do be wary of their nomenclature and ensure that they include tree spreads.)

Photograph the site at this initial visit, and sit down and envisage your design and planting plan there and then. You should not wait until you have a plan on a drawing board or screen. It might be weeks before you are able to do this so, if you have to wait for a survey, decide on the spot whether you want it formal or curvy, for instance - and make notes and a sketch for yourself and the new clients' file. If the site is abroad and you do not know whether you will come back, or even if it is only two hours' drive away, get the facts down immediately and take as many photographs as you can.

Get back to your car and fill in that checklist immediately.

Sample project: The brief

"Oh," the client says, "I have made a list of all the things we would like you to work into the garden plan; there are a few photos too of things we like." Obvious shots of 'heritage gardens' appear while I look bleakly at their north-facing back garden! But I like this approach, and usually it's helpful, though clients often need reminding that their ideas have to be in scale.

For this example, I want to take you to a site at the edge of Ashdown Forest, in the south-east of England. The garden is surrounded by enormous oak trees. Approached down a steep hill, the dark-brick single-storey house sits in a clearing, with a double garage on the left. I think I can see the front door but my first impression is that it would be nice if the main entrance was more obvious.

I am greeted by my clients, a husband and wife in their 30s or early 40s. They have two sons at school, aged about 10 and 12. I later discover that my client is a broadcasting editor, who is in constant touch with my nephew who is a broadcaster. It's a small world, as they say.

I do not think that my clients have lived in the house all that long and until now have been expending their energies on altering and decorating that. But the garden space at the rear of the house is pretty dilapidated and they now want to do something with it. The house is in fact L-shaped and the courtyard feel of the garden space is reinforced by the ground stepping up on the two other sides of the house. The house was obviously excavated out of its site and an ominous hump on the one side is, I hope, topsoil and not heavy clay.

Great oaks marking the edge of the forest are on the south and west of the site. The clients and their children have a quick exit route down the north side of the house, where they cycle through the forest to get to the local railway station. With forests go wildlife, and deer might be a problem in this garden or could be – any vegetables will have to be caged in order to protect them.

The clients' wish list

My clients have produced a very good wish list asking for a sense of privacy and seclusion – as the north side of the property looks down upon other rear gardens. Simple, unfussy natural planting is called for, not too rustic, together with constructions that are made from natural materials.

They sensibly ask for more turning space on entering the drive and, sure enough, they do want to make the main entrance to the house more obvious. So we are thinking along the same lines. They also request the following:

- a summerhouse or similar structure
- more outside seating to make use of the sunny spots between the trees
- some water
- for the children: some shaded play areas, swings, sandpit, a treehouse, and spaces to play ball games
- a vegetable plot
- planting to be low-maintenance
- simple, flowering, unfussy, natural planting that blends in
- drought-tolerant planting.

This seems like a pretty good brief to me.

I was not able to measure up this site and I would need to take levels, as there are humps and bumps everywhere (mostly clay, the client advises). So we discuss having a survey done, to which the clients agree.

I still go outside and sketch for myself the way in which I would like to develop the site. This is really based upon which areas get sunlight and which do not, and what is level and what is not. I photograph the area and talk through rough ideas. I am dying to get the survey done and set to work.

"I photograph the area and talk through rough ideas. I am dying to get the survey done and and set to work."

Opposite All these notes and images go into the new file to await the survey to which my client has agreed. This might take six weeks, and another visit to the site might not be possible when it arrives – so get down plenty of detail at this stage.

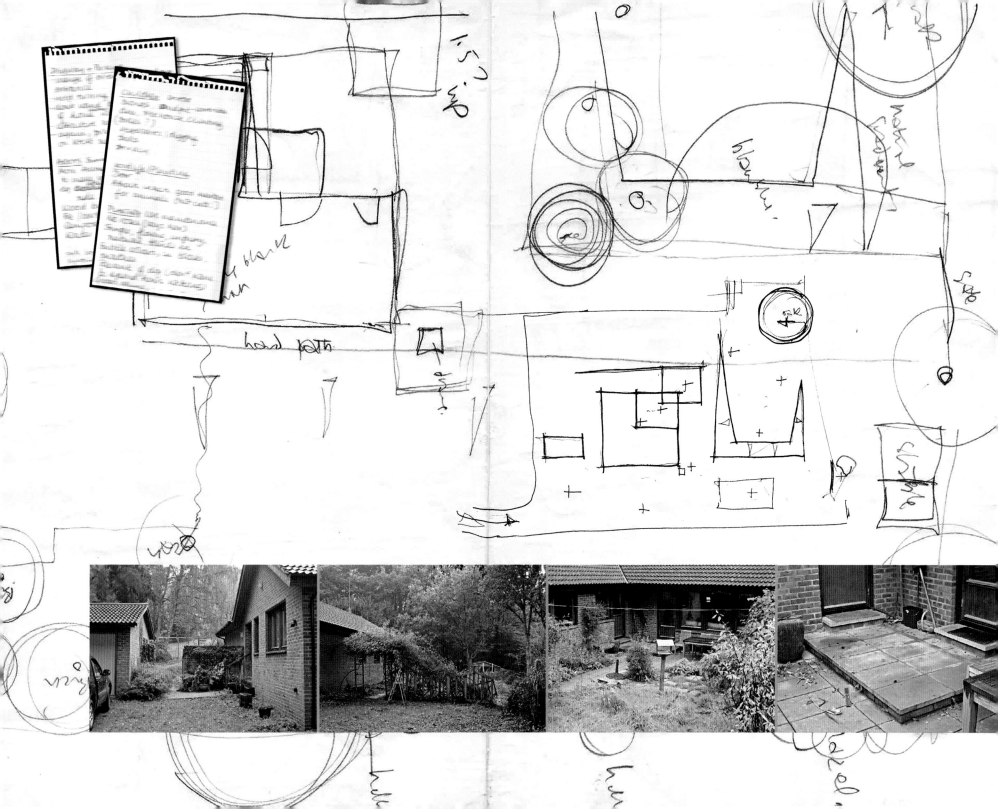

Right: It would take a week for my assistant and myself to measure up a site like this, so while the client probably paid a three-figure sum for this painstaking survey – he has an accurate record of his site for posterity, and I have something really exciting to work upon. The garage and the house are at the centre; all the trees are clearly marked and listed with the spread of their canopies. There is little in full sunlight. Contours are clearly marked, and spot levels given where I indicated I would like them in my letter to the surveyor. The north point is to the bottom of the survey. There is a mound of clay on the western corner of the house, and a small hillock to the south. The gateway to the forest path to the station is on the south also. The drive enters the site from the east.

Obtaining a survey

Once I have permission from my client to have their property surveyed, I contact my favourite surveyor, who does not live too far away. (It is as well to get to know someone whom you can trust to do a good job for you, and does not mind travelling.) This site, I would suggest, is probably a day's work. On this time basis I can quote how much the survey will be to my client. Once approved, I send a hand-drawn plan of the site along with the address and contact number to the surveyor and let him get on with it, though I try to establish the date on which he will carry out the work. If I was really efficient I would send an ordnance survey of the location and site.

With this information I also indicate where I want levels taken – and mark the spots to be taken from a datum point – which is usually a doorstep or something fixed. A surveyor might just give you spot levels, but I ask for actual contours to be drawn based on these levels, so that the whole site is covered.

If there are large existing trees, on-site levels are important so that, if you anticipate using machinery, you know to work well away from the tree canopy overhang. You will need not only tree girths on your survey but the area of the tree canopies as well. This way you will then see from the survey what is in sun, and what is not.

Of course if you are hot from design school you will know how to make your own survey with laser equipment and the like. There was a time…! But on a site like this which is quite complicated, because I need all the other information it contains, I prefer to use a professional.

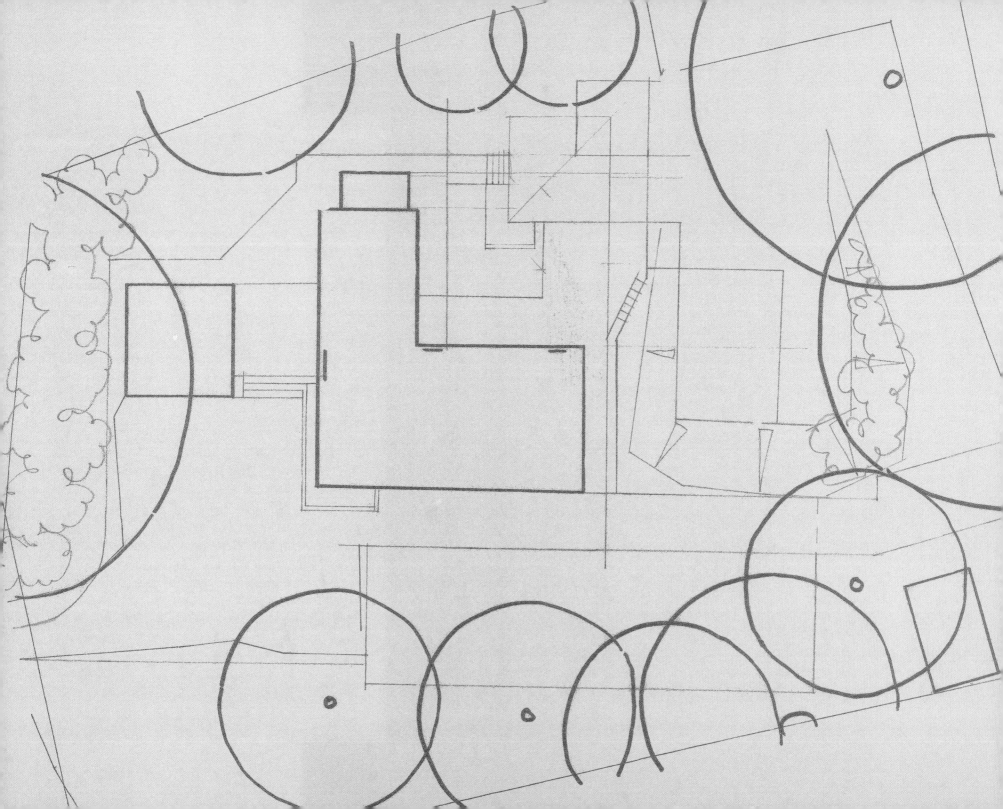

Sample project: Meeting the brief

Because of the varying levels and the existing features of this site, I begin in the rear courtyard, which is the core of what this garden is all about, building up in more detail the geometry of the sketch I made on the site. Bearing in mind both the orientation of the site and what is out of the shade of trees, it is fairly obvious terraces must be placed so that they become a feature – to be seen from inside the house as well – and where the vegetable patch should go (on the raised area at the side of the house).

Removing the hump of clay from the north of the house and grading the slope will create a good kick-about area for the boys, along with a grassy lawn at the top of the garden under the huge oak as an additional area for play equipment, keeping it out of the way and yet just visible from the house and terrace.

There will need to be retaining walls of some sort to hold the terraces, probably in cost-effective organic wood, as requested. By using retaining walls, instead of the current rocky banks, I can also enhance the sound of running water from a water feature.

Evolving the design

The clients asked for a very natural garden, which to me presupposes soft curves, but the siting of the house within the regular shape of the site leaves little space for this and so I will have to rely on plant material to soften the final effect. In addition, the overhanging trees have such a strong form that the overall garden design will need a strength to it.

Discussion with the clients also suggested connecting the front door to the garage with a built extension, which is fine and would not negate my proposal for much wider steps to the door, working with strong planting to soften the 'brickiness' of the end wall that you see as you come down the drive. I would formalise and enlarge the entrance forecourt with a path round the garage to allow everyone's cycles to be wheeled round the back, and then probably dumped on the ground! Rubbish bins can also go round the side here.

I have now roughly blocked out the areas of the garden plan, and next go on to fill in the details. At this point, I could enter the details into the computer, but I still believe that the basic concept should be drawn by hand.

Left This drawing would probably be an overlay on the survey, roughly blocking in where the main garden should be in the angle of the house, stepping up to the highest point. I sited a caged (deer-proof) vegetable area to the right of the house and the boys' play area, with an enlarged entrance and forecourt on the left.

Below I am beginning to develop in sketch form the feeling I would like to achieve as the garden builds up towards the large oaks beyond the courtyard. The L-shaped house will look into this area. It will be heavily used as well with raised paved areas for a table and sunbathing.

Scale drawing

This is my presentation drawing to the client and this is what sells the concept. I trust my drawing will be accurate, since I worked from the dimensions given in the survey, but it is a concept I am selling not a working design. I try to include as much dimension into my drawing as possible by using different thicknesses of pen. The house, the garage and the oak trees will obviously dominate and their drawn lines will be thickest. My first line will define my pavings. Plantings and other features will be shown by using an intermediate thickness of line. So far, I have scarcely mentioned plant material, other than the existing shrubs and trees. I am preparing a stage setting for them. This first plan indicates levels, locates seating areas, parking spaces and paving areas, along with any other features.

The drawing does not provide a multi-coloured presentation. In fact, I often only colour in the grassed areas. As soon as one gets into heavy colouring and shadows the time I can allot to this stage starts to be eaten away, and we are running a business. I once learned my lesson on over-colouring a plan when I was asked to provide eight additional copies for the members of the board. I think it helps to lightly shade in any evergreen material, but I would do little more.

I write on my plan to explain my intention and this makes the drawing easier to read. By all means, expand your plan notes into a report, particularly if you are sending your proposals by post and are not presenting them personally. Always include a North point, which makes sense of the drawing, as well as, of course, an indication of the scale of the drawing. To fill out my presentation pages, I also provide sketches which include cut-outs taken from digital photograph prints . By overlaying the photographs with sketches, you'll find that you will create images that appeal to the clients and explain your intentions almost more than the plan.

I condition myself to wait for the clients' response to this drawing. Some are on the phone the next day saying "Yes, what is the next stage?" With others I wait and wait, and eventually I hear that they have been on holiday, or they have doubts, which I am always happy to discuss. This plan was a proposal only, and can be altered. But not by too much.

If the client definitely dislikes the plan, then it is the designer who has failed – I may have forgotten something or misheard or misread the signs. I will always offer to alter and redraw the plan, but fortunately this total re-draw does not happen too often.

Left An indication to the client of how he might enlarge the steps to the front door to make more of it. And then extending one of the treads to become the coping to a new planter would partially help to soften the rather daunting end wall of the house as you enter the site by car. Planting could also extend across the garden to divide parking space from kickabout lawn area.

Right The plan I present to my client with annotations for the proposed design.

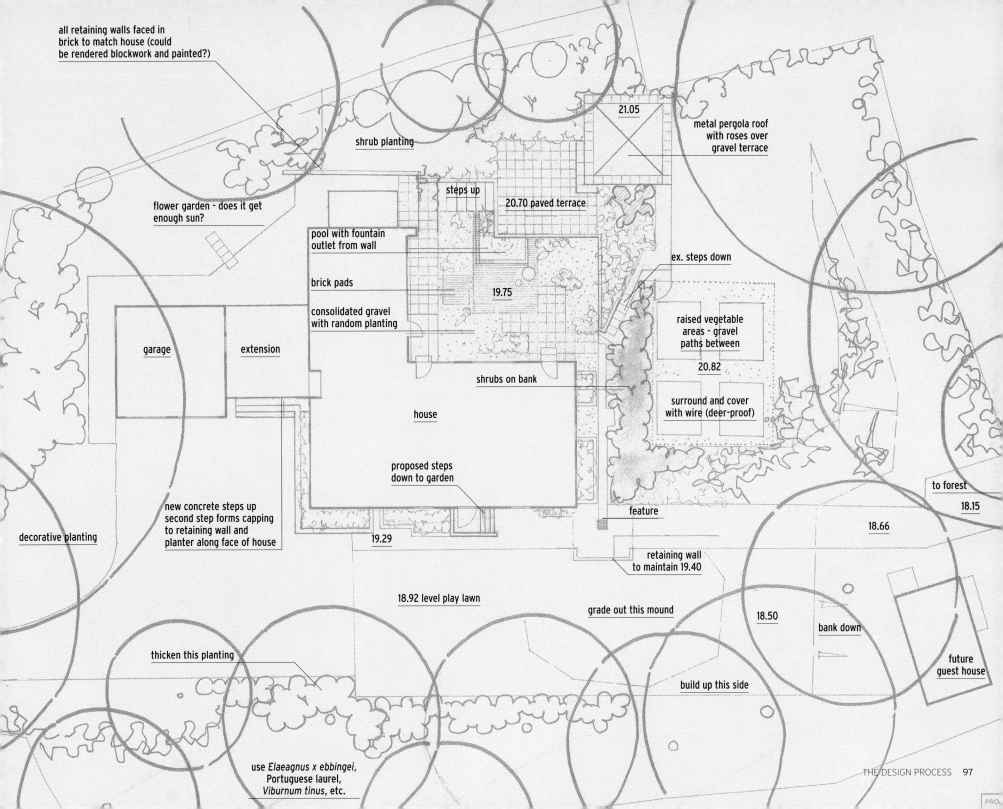

all retaining walls faced in brick to match house (could be rendered blockwork and painted?)

shrub planting

21.05

metal pergola roof with roses over gravel terrace

flower garden - does it get enough sun?

steps up

20.70 paved terrace

pool with fountain outlet from wall

ex. steps down

brick pads

consolidated gravel with random planting

19.75

raised vegetable areas - gravel paths between

20.82

garage

extension

shrubs on bank

surround and cover with wire (deer-proof)

house

proposed steps down to garden

to forest

18.15

feature

new concrete steps up second step forms capping to retaining wall and planter along face of house

18.66

decorative planting

19.29

retaining wall to maintain 19.40

18.92 level play lawn

grade out this mound

18.50

bank down

thicken this planting

build up this side

future guest house

use *Elaeagnus x ebbingei*, Portuguese laurel, *Viburnum tinus*, etc.

Proceeding

If you still hear nothing from the clients for a long while, send the bill - that usually elicits a response! The best possible scenario is that the clients are excited and get in touch to say that they want to go ahead.

So what next? Depending upon the complexity of the site, now might also be the time to ask to have a detailed survey drawn up, particularly to help with measuring levels, because your next drawings should include working details. The sketch plan now needs to be turned into reality.

With the sketch plan in mind, you can now discuss with your clients the hard landscaping - which materials are appropriate for terraces, paths, pavings, retaining walls, and so on. Some aspects might need subcontracting out to specialists - for example the swimming pool, the tennis court, water features, or even lighting.

The next stage

Also, maintain the discussion over job procedure with your clients at this stage. This covers when the work should be done, how many contractors should be approached for prices, whether you are to supervise the construction and how and when you will be paid. Have a good discussion preferably with both husband and wife, or partners, all together. That way, you know exactly where you are going.

Depending on the size of your site, you may now need to enlarge your plan. Where I have any problems over detail or for a detailed planting plan, I would work at a scale of 1:50 (1/4"-1'0" in the US), and I may enlarge any portion of the original plan which was at a scale of 1:200 or 1:100. As we move into the more specific structural work, computer-aided design begins to come into its own (see pages 80-1). The point of these drawings is to clarify in your own mind what you are proposing, and to make it easier for a contractor to price the work and eventually to build it. Of course, we all come to a point where we don't know how to build a certain element - you cannot possibly know everything - but there is usually someone around from whom you can seek advice. Never be too proud to ask, and I find that most people are only too happy to help.

By producing a projection (see right), you begin to realise some of the problems that you have set yourself in the two-dimensional plan.

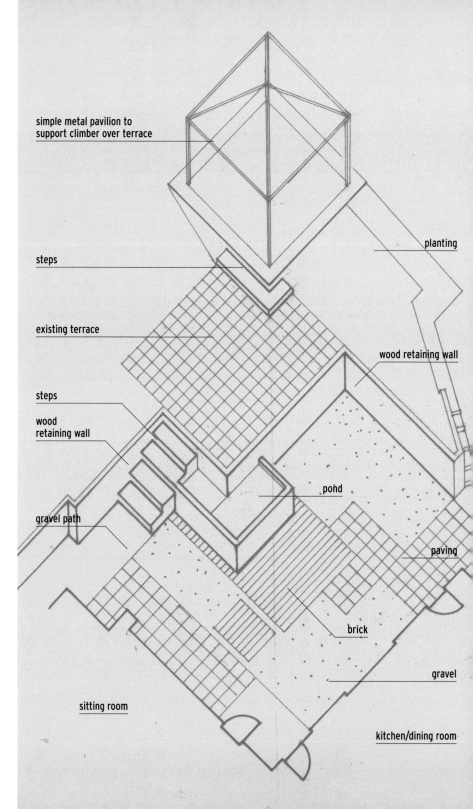

simple metal pavilion to support climber over terrace

planting

steps

existing terrace

wood retaining wall

steps

wood retaining wall

pond

gravel path

paving

brick

gravel

sitting room

kitchen/dining room

The right expertise

In the particular job I am illustrating here I had wanted to build retaining walls in brick to echo the house but my clients prefer timber – it being cheaper and probably more appropriate in their forest setting. However, I have never built walls in wood or incorporated water into such a structure, so I needed to seek advice. A contractor friend e-mailed me his specification for building wooden sleeper retaining walls, which is a help, but I still could not see how to lose the edges of the pool liner – so I drew up the pond and step detail, supporting a timber sleeper main wall, with a step riser and pool surround in brick. Drawing up these sorts of problematic details really makes you think the problem through.

A staged approach

The clients in this particular case are very happy with the plan and detail, but they want to do the work in stages over a period of time. This seems a perfectly reasonable approach where funds are limited and time is at a premium. Planting on this job is pretty minimal anyway because of the overhanging shade and, no doubt, dryness. And, if truth be told, I do not mind not having to do a planting detail at all.

    The clients are keeping in touch as the job proceeds.

"... there is usually someone around from whom you can seek advice. Never be too proud to ask, and I find that most people are only too happy to help."

Left This is an axonometric projection which brings levels into play. That third dimension suddenly jumps into life.

Right An elevation showing the wooden retaining walls, at the back of the pond. If I had retained the timber for the pond surround I could find a way to conceal the butyl rubber liner which holds the water – so I have suggested a brick pond with a coping to match the paving, because its overhang would conceal the liner. Steps behind the pond are also in brick.

Design case study: A one-visit consultation

Sometimes I may visit a site only once, particularly when the site is abroad. In this case, I was visiting my client's in-laws, and as a throw-away line I was told that their daughter and her husband had just bought a new house close by and would I like to go and see it this evening? "Now," I think, "what do they mean? Do I take the invitation literally, or is this the beginning of another job?"

People are always asking me what my favourite garden is, and I find it very difficult to answer, because after all these years I still look at and analyse every garden I see; I can't help it. So visiting a garden is not exactly restful, but I also need to be very careful when looking at a new house and garden to make sure that the owners want my advice because, inevitably, I analyse gardens as second nature.

This couple do want advice in a big way and, as usual, I shoot my mouth off, saying something about the drive being in the wrong place, cutting the garden in half, and suggest that the drive would be better nearer the garage and front door, particularly since they are in a North American location and snow will need to be cleared. Then I look at the shape, and the forecourt, and whether a swimming pool would fit or not, how the terrace provided by the developers could be enlarged, and so on.

So a social visit became a drawing. I am told they are just doing the new drive at the moment. Provided they don't hit rock below the surface, I hope to see it finished next time I am in the area.

Above This would be the view from the house down to a road crossing, though beyond that is a fine lake. The existing drive seen on the plan (**left**) comes up from this crossing and cuts across the garden at the front of the house.

Opposite, top A subsequent and more detailed layout of the terrace and contouring round the house. The old drive will be planted out to create a more intimate, wild type of layout.

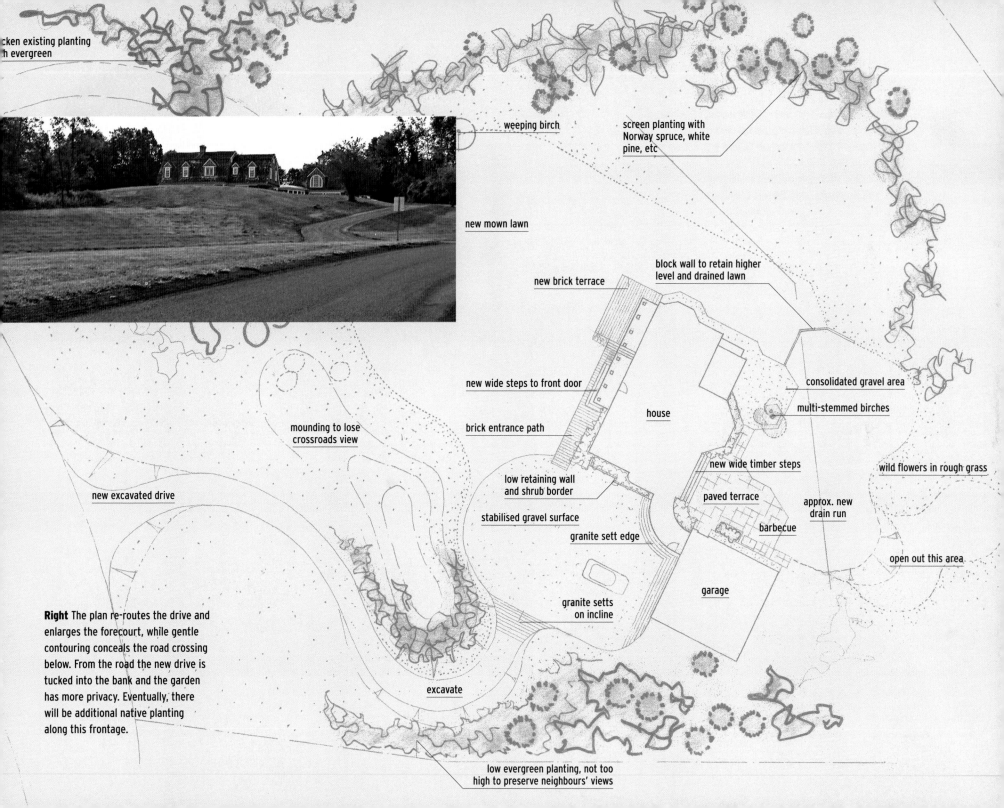

cken existing planting
h evergreen

weeping birch

screen planting with Norway spruce, white pine, etc

new mown lawn

new brick terrace

block wall to retain higher level and drained lawn

new wide steps to front door

consolidated gravel area

multi-stemmed birches

house

brick entrance path

mounding to lose crossroads view

new wide timber steps

wild flowers in rough grass

low retaining wall and shrub border

paved terrace

new excavated drive

approx. new drain run

stabilised gravel surface

barbecue

granite sett edge

open out this area

granite setts on incline

garage

Right The plan re-routes the drive and enlarges the forecourt, while gentle contouring conceals the road crossing below. From the road the new drive is tucked into the bank and the garden has more privacy. Eventually, there will be additional native planting along this frontage.

excavate

low evergreen planting, not too high to preserve neighbours' views

Below A plan of the new house and its adjacent barn. Drainage seemed of primary importance, which of course the architect thought about, but subsequent hard surfacing might provide more of a problem. A central gully should be part of the paving pattern, with gravel over drainage pipes surrounding the house as well.

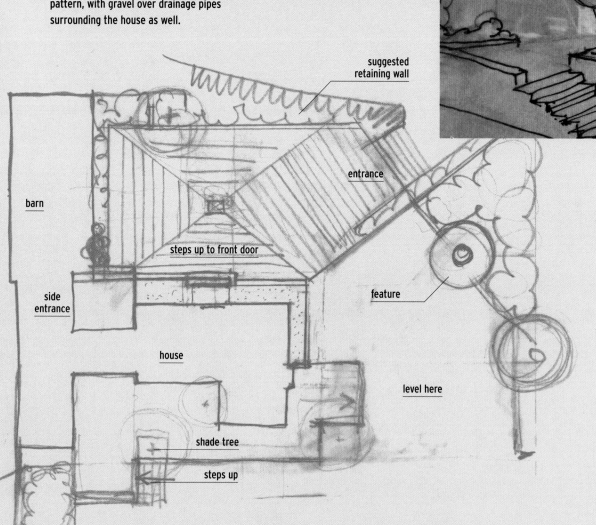

suggested retaining wall

entrance

barn

steps up to front door

side entrance

feature

house

level here

shade tree

steps up

Above A quick sketch idea for a terrace at the rear of the house. The retaining wall is slightly raised so that it can be used as a place to sit. Wide stone steps lead down to a rough grass meadow. This is a south-facing terrace and I have proposed a tree for some shade.

Design case study: A quick visit

I first worked for these clients about 20 years ago and it is always flattering to be asked again. The husband and wife are now building onto an existing barn; down-sizing, I believe it is called. A quick visit is required since the builders working on the house want to clear the site and start to create levels the following week.

The house and forecourt are approached downhill, so they are obviously going to catch water. The house is below this area by four or five steps, and provision needs to be made to prevent this becoming a problem. Although the builder had taken steps towards catching water, I still suggest they surround the house with gravel with drains in it. Also I am adamant that if a central drain has to go in the forecourt it has to centre on the front door, with a paving pattern working round it. (Off-centre drains and manhole covers are a garden designer's and landscaper's nightmare.)

The steps to the front door need to be made wider, since the big barn window dominates the area, rivalled by a gap between the two buildings.

Much could be corrected by planting. A retaining wall, rather than a bank, on the opposite side of the courtyard to the front door could contain a good-sized specimen tree, which I would import and locate before the retaining wall is completed.

At the rear of the house, the worked garden is to be minimal. I propose a terrace, to create a ha-ha effect. From it there would be a 2-metre drop with wide and gentle steps down to what would be a rough, mown area bordering cultivated fields. The terrace would need a slight walled up-stand, to prevent people from falling off it, but also making a wonderful casual seat. The terrace and wall would continue to the side of the house, gradually diminishing to a level for both terrace and grass.

The client rang me to say that his architect had everything buttoned up, and he had gone out on a limb, asking me to visit. "Oh well," I thought, "Nothing ventured, nothing gained."

They paid up, too!

Right The proposed paved yard entrance, with planting masses used to balance out the scale of the barn window. A silhouette of trees was also suggested between the house and barn planted in the area beyond.

My planting technique

It must seem, I appreciate, that garden designers are less keen on planting than on constructing, since the planting always gets left until last. This premise, however, is far from the truth. It is only when the thinking, the planning and the building are completed that you can consider what to plant. It seems perverse of course, for it is the planting of a job and its maintenance that most people consider first, only realising after a while how the space itself works and of what and how it is constructed.

The reality is that one takes on board the planting – if not in the job itself then certainly by analysing the gardens or countryside around the prospective site. Why? Because it is the existing vegetation that tells the designer so much about the soil, and moisture levels; and it is the existing vegetation that defines the shaded and possibly dry areas. If it is a new site you can probably surmise what grew there once from a look beyond its bounds. In short, it is the planting that defines the character of the land, and it is within this that all subsequent planning (with reference to the house, its style, orientation and building material) has to take place. And after that you'll want an overview of not the planting of the site but its physical elements, the services: the drive, the garage location, and so forth. But most importantly your plans should have addressed the client's brief. And in terms of planting (though not necessarily much else), clients are often very vocal. The showcase gardens, those everyone has heard of, which are open to the public or featured on TV, get a regular mention, but we have to 'get real'. Your client went to one, or even all of these places once – did they go again in winter, do they know what maintenance facility and what water availability these gardens have, for instance?

Get real!

All such practical points need to be talked through with the client. The very first questions to ask are: are they gardeners; how much time can they spend gardening or do they plan to employ a gardener, and if so, do they know the hourly rate for a gardener in their area? The responses to all these points will help to define what the planting will be like. Only then should you move on to the details of

Right I want my plantings to describe the character of the place, to appear as if they have always been part of that environment. If you choose native material, there is every likelihood that it will thrive.

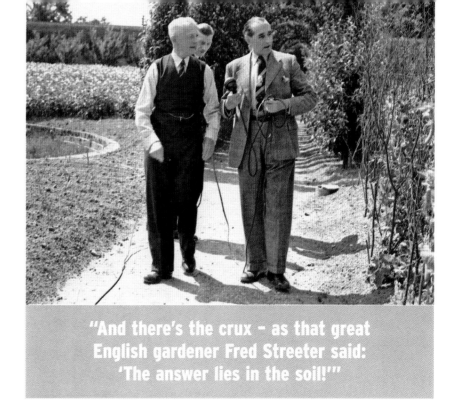

the planting. Among other things you might discuss whether they want, for instance, herbaceous plantings or mixed borders with annuals in pots; a vast lawn or herbs and vegetable plots; a compost area; glazing and whether it will be opened and closed manually or automatically; a cold frame; hard standing; water butts. In addition, lighting, water and power points need to be considered, and so on. Each site will be different, as will each garden designer's solution, addressing the problems of orientation, wind, sun, shade and soil. And there's the crux – as that great English gardener (with over 60 years actively gardening) Fred Streeter said: "The answer lies in the soil!"

Planting a new site

One of the first jobs on a new site is to clear it of its weed. The better the job you do, the easier your life will become in future. Ground elder, bindweed, celandines and the like, if not initially cleared are devilishly hard to get rid of subsequently since they gets into plants, which have to be lifted and cleaned.

If you have brambles and scrub to clear, cut them down and then spray. Now I am not a chemical user generally since they are lethal in destroying all the micro-organisms of the surface and vital few inches of topsoil, but *in extremis*, needs, I think sometimes must. In smaller areas hand digging – more than once is to be recommended (it gets easier each time as the roots become smaller). Other techniques include blanketing a site with a plastic sheet for a season, but it looks so awful. Do not be conned into just rotovating your site - it isn't nearly enough for you to simply chop up the roots and further distribute them round your site.

When the decks are cleared, and the design has been marked out – even built – it is time to start to think about plant material in detail – though the designer should have had broad ideas all along. Try to define realistically in your mind the look you want to achieve:

- Is it the flowery cottage garden or a green continental semi-formal look?
- Is it the full clipped, balanced formal layout or more of a loose, shrubby green look?
- Or is it a definite wild approach, in which case do you like the new perennial and grass look, or the wild flower meadow (and have you read about creating it)?

"And there's the crux – as that great English gardener Fred Streeter said: 'The answer lies in the soil!'"

Going with the flow

If you live in either hotter or colder areas than the temperate latitudes I have been discussing, go with your climate. If you've moved from New Jersey to Tucson, leave New Jersey behind - flowering cherries and lawns are out, they both look wrong, and they won't survive. This is where a little design advice comes in handy.

The same applies at the other end of the spectrum, too: don't try to push your luck with exotic rhododendrons, for instance - when they don't make it through winter, it becomes an expensive hobby. You won't get much evergreen, other than coniferous species which are adapted to the cold, and you need to think about snow damage.

So, how do you start to select your plants? Again it was teaching that made me try to rationalise the process. I find it much easier to categorise plants for their uses, not just the colour of their flowers. I still divide my plants into categories and functions. And these are: the specials, the skeleton, the infill, the pretties, and the flotsam.

The specials

These are often the trees that exist already on site. They might be enormous, casting deep shade and causing the site to be very dry. In new developments they may well have a preservation order upon them.

Before tampering with large trees, particularly in urban and suburban locations, check their status with the authorities to ensure there are no tree preservation orders. And if none applies, remember too that the tree gives you shade and a cartload of autumn leaves, provides a wonderful screen/backdrop for your neighbours, and is even the pivotal tree in the whole development. Wars are started for more trifling reasons than tampering with that tree!

Older trees anyway in tighter locations, need a fairly regular inspection for disease. Always use a qualified and insured tree surgeon for any tree work, especially where it involves climbing.

Your existing specials might be much lighter or be even a massed silver birch group, whose trunks make a lovely backdrop to your development.

Or if you are starting from scratch you will probably plant your specials.

These will probably be trees with individual merit, that stand out from other, possibly larger, trees that you put in to build up your skeleton for wind shelter or to provide a screen. Examples are the Magnolia for spring flower, the Albizzia for shade, the Cercidiphyllum for fall colour, Koelreuteria for summer flowers and in winter the peeling stems of *Acer griseum*. You will not want too many specials or the mix becomes indigestible.

Whether you like it or not, some trees are what I call pushy and will become special whether you like it or not. Anything purple is pretty demanding – laburnum I find fairly antisocial, its spring colour being so strong, and pink cherries in spring seem to stand out like a sore thumb to me. Other personal prejudices I have are tree ferns, and what I would call Surrey conifers. I've got

Below left A mixed woodland planting, in which different trees will become special in different seasons. Conifers and silver birch stems read well in winter. **Below** The value of evergreens cannot be overstated – here a fine specimen of yew (*Taxus baccata*).

Opposite A row of planes (*Platanus* spp.) creates an interesting special feature in an urban situation. Eventual top pruning of their heads will be necessary, however. **Far right** A Japanese maple (*Acer* spp.) in autumn becomes very special.

used to monkey puzzles (*Araucaria*) where there are woods of them in parts of South America, and to eucalyptus, which are wonderful in Australia - and that's the crunch: they look good in their native environment, but I would question their use elsewhere.

The other thing to check when selecting your specials is their ultimate size. Trees grow fast, and we have a curious loathing at having to cut them down. So check on their growth rate, on their height in say 10 years and then 20, and their width as well. We've all seen the roadside bungalow absolutely swamped by the 25m spread of a weeping willow and can only surmise at what its roots are doing to the foundations - so think ahead. Any catalogue or plantsman will tell you these things.

Spare a thought as well for the tree roots near buildings. Different trees have differing root systems and react differently to different soils - do check.

The skeleton

I get to the bones after placing my key or special plants – which need not necessarily be trees, perhaps the word pivotal would be better, for one yucca in a bed of perennials becomes just that. To my mind, what alarms many people looking at newer grassier plantings is that they lack these pivotal elements, and if they are wrongly placed as individuals, grasses can become spotty in an overall arrangement.

What steadies plantings down, provides a backdrop, a windbreak and/or a visual or noise screen are the very useful range of plants that I call skeleton plant material.

To work all year round, skeleton plants should of course be evergreen. In more northerly climates these may be coniferous, pines or spruces, in more temperate areas yew (*Taxus* spp), or box (*Buxus*) will do the trick. In Mediterranean climates I would go for *Pittosporum tobira* or the casuarina.

These plants you select for a function; they are not intended to be decorative (though they are). As well as providing screen and/or shelter these are the basic plants which I would use to build up the backbone of my design.

I always say to students that it is more important to have this range of material at your fingertips, rather than an unnecessarily large vocabulary of perennials, for without this vital backdrop, they will look nothing.

I also point out that you are often asked to provide a working layout, including these basics; and not necessarily a decorative infill. Quite often clients want to do that themselves (irritatingly!). The skeleton range I can work with in gardens in Britain is not large, although within each species there are lots of varieties. Know your viburnums – both evergreen and deciduous – they are terrific. Elaeagnus are, I believe, good; pyracanthus have prickles, flowers and fruit; the cotoneasters are a large range, from ground hugging to small tree; the semi-evergreen, more than the fully so, rhododendrons are excellent in acid soils; escallonias are good by the sea, as are certain hebes, particularly *Hebe brachysiphon*, and *H. salicifolia*.

Above left Yew (*Taxus* spp.) and variegated box (*Buxus* spp.) create strong bones at the rear of this mixed shrub planting.

Left The sharp, thick stems of yuccas contrast with glossy oval banana foliage in this tropical garden.

The infill

Once I have established the bones of my design – beginning to make my two-dimensional layout plan into a three-dimensional reality – I start to infill first with decorative shrubs and later with perennials. The grasses come along with the perennials, both of which I like to use in broad swathes, although this will depend upon the scale of the site and space available.

I am not now planting in prepared borders necessarily, I could be building up my canvases in a gravel, or mulched area (which I would then top up), for in my selection of plant material I am increasingly concerned with sustainability. By that I mean using plant material that is happy in the conditions provided for it, without the necessity of altering the soil's pH value – its acidity or alkalinity – though I may have altered the soil's water-holding capacity to retain moisture by amending it with organic matter. And I may well subsequently mulch over the top of the soil to retain the moisture in it.

It was noticeable in England during the prolonged drought period what did, and did not do well, what wilted after a hot day and what did not. Anything with large leaves tended to flop, owing to transpiration. Fine leaves, hairy leaves and grey or waxy leaves are all adaptations to heat and are modifications to the plant's physiognomy. Hydrangeas were devils at the end of the day. Someone said that a plant that has wilted at the end of a hot day is fine, if it is still wilted in the morning, you may have a problem with it!

Traditional English shrubs such as lilac (*Syringa*), mock orange (*Philadelphus*), elder (*Sambucus*) and shrub roses all survive fairly well through extremes of temperature. Much Mediterranean material does well in more northerly latitudes too, though the plants do require good drainage. Many of the plants and herbs from warmer climates survive in their native environment in very poor soils; they do not have excessively long winters with damp roots for months. That, I believe, is a killer.

Above right *Philadelphus* or mock orange makes an admirable infill shrub in a temperate climate.

Right Low-growing evergreens and semi-evergreens provide infill and a backdrop to seasonal shows of colourful blooms.

Try to plant in groups of at least two or three of each kind of shrub. If you use a single variety it becomes a special - if you use lots of single varieties together it becomes a mess. Start off at least with this is mind.

When selecting trees, shrubs or perennials, any plant in fact, have a nurseryman's catalogue to hand, which not only has a good description of ultimate height and width, but foliage and berry as well as flower. Don't forget that flower tends to be transitory, so ask yourself whether a buddleia is worth having for the other fifty weeks of the year, for instance - does its shape and foliage make a positive addition to the garden?

The current vogue for perennials seems to be at the cost of shrubby material which I think is a pity. The temperate climate allows us to grow a miraculous range of woody plants (though you won't need them all in your plot), which can enhance the garden all year round.

The pretties

I would really like to amend this description. The range of plants I start to select for my next grouping are the ones at 'the front of the border', in old-world gardening terms; and in the new, they are core plants along with grasses. I have made a plea previously for more woody plants in these newer plantings, so that I still have interest in my groupings. I can't become lyrical about grass heads on a wet November day and it's noticeable that the photographers are only out on frosty mornings. But begonias and hellebores, for instance, mix well and love the damp even though they may be lost in summer.

The newer mixed plantings do look handsome through summer, but they are not miraculously maintenance-free. Plants and grasses need dividing from time to time and watch out for the self-seeders. Make sure your area is weed free too before planting, since ground elder amongst the perennials is a nightmare to eradicate.

Meadow plantings tend to be more of biennials and annuals amongst grasses. Their flowerings are spectacular, but then you have a hay field. Entire books are written on establishing meadows - take note, they are not for the faint-hearted.

Opposite (top) One of my favourite range of plants is the hellebore. This is *Helleborus niger*, the Christmas rose, one of the oldest cultivated plants in Britain.

Opposite (below) Meadow-style plantings can look glorious with their summer blooms amongst grasses, but in maintenance terms they are not the easy option.

Below The newer, gentler, plant association in gravel: grasses (*Miscanthus sinensis*) with red-hot pokers (*Kniphofia caulescens*), *Helleborus corsicus* and *Iris foetidissima*.

The flotsam

My final group includes bulbs that can be planted through the perennials perhaps, along with the lilies on the terrace and the ferns in the shade. It also takes in all the ground-covering plants that are so important to help reinforce the job of mulch in conserving moisture in the soil. I would add all the forms of climbing plant – the self-clingers, the twisters and those that need supporting. (Note: if you are doing a planting for someone else, you will need to specify supports where necessary.)

I suppose that pots of annuals come into this category as well. More and more I see groupings of pots being stabilised by the odd box ball or piece of topiary. These, I think, steady down what can all too easily develop into a mass of pots and terrace – and this is particularly so in a small area. Use subjects that are drought-hardy for this purpose.

Finally, a tip I tell students when doing planting plans: if you have not got room for all the names in Latin (some of which are long) then either your scale is too small, or quite probably you have got too much in. Remember: it is not your garden, this is for someone else to maintain. So take out half of what you first thought of, and double up the numbers of what remains.

Opposite A true flotsam in the spring border which includes tulip species, hellebores and bellis species.

Below, left to right While I list the flotsam last in the order of priorities in which I select my material to build up a concept, it often reads as the most important, eye-catching element of it. The wisteria is very beautiful in late spring. Earlier will be all the tulips, and following them a whole exciting range of alliums, which retain their flower heads right into summer.

The planting plan: Planting styles

I have outlined the categories in my mind, and how I use them sequentially to build up my planting plan. It's worth keeping in mind the whole time that repetition is good to quieten too riotous a concept (see page 52). Depending on the site I am planting, I try to triangulate my repeats – very broadly, and to soften a hard edge, where practical, I plant on both sides of the dividing line.

When cutting back on existing planting, I like to let the plants breathe, by which I mean not have too solid a mass of growing material of the same height – this is where layering comes in (see page 52).

There are no doubt many styles of plant association, dependent upon climate and different vegetation. But my categories for Britain might be: clipped and formal, semi-formal, architectural, traditional massing/cottagey, the newer, grassier/perennial look, the gravelly look, and playing with colour.

Below, left A clipped and semi-formal look, using box (*Buxus* spp.) and yew (*Taxus* spp.), with, behind, softer splaying plant material.

Below, centre The gravelly look, in which perennials and biennials self-seed and overwinter, to appear the following spring.

Below, right Traditional massing woody material mixed with perennials. *Hydrangea arborescens* 'Annabelle' is backed with *Romneya coulteri*, the California tree poppy. In front are white agapanthus, with the seedheads of fennel on the right.

Opposite, top left A formal planting with yew and, in the distance, pleached limes (*Tilia* spp.)

Opposite, top right An architectural mix of New Zealand flax (*Phormium tenax*), eleagnus, yucca, and the white heads of the hogweed.

Opposite, bottom left Grasses with Euphorbia growing in gravel, the wilder way.

Opposite, bottom right Pink tulips, here contrasted with the grey architectural leaves of the cardoon (*Cynara cardunculus*).

Planting case study: For keen gardeners

Newly built in a mellow stone this house in the Midlands of England stands alone, surrounded by fields just outside a village. The house was built by a retired farmer and his wife. He is keen on vegetables and she on growing in general.

The house faces west where it is approached via a track and you enter the garden over a ha-ha and cattle grid. The view is towards an open meadow with clumps of trees, under which on the day I saw it sheep were gently grazing. I thought the scene idyllic.

A traditional garden was called for in such a setting and my plan was fairly straightforward, with a flower garden, a covered terrace, a vegetable garden, and an orchard. My clients were very keen on shrub roses, and had some to move from their existing garden – for they had not yet moved into this new house.

The plan was to pave the front door area, on which there was a bench seat, and the covered terrace on the south of the house. The rest of the surfaces were to be of consolidated local gravel with a boarded edging.

The orchard area was to have paths mown through a rougher grass surround to a selection of fruit trees.

The flower garden was to be cottagey, a mixture of favourite shrubs with perennials – the client gave me a very precise list. The area to the north of the house, was to minimise the tennis court surround and generally soften the approach to the main door of the house off its rear car turning space. A small pavilion creates a visual stop to the entrance drive.

Left My clients' house is a new one, but it stands in a mature setting with plenty of full-grown trees, so the proposed traditional planting would help to make house and garden look very much in keeping.

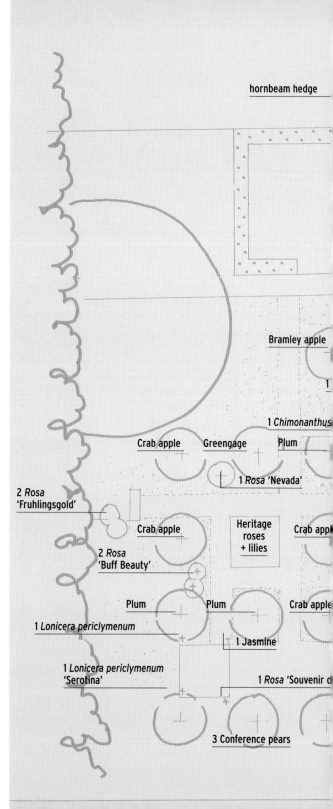

hornbeam hedge

Bramley apple

1 *Chimonanthus*

Crab apple   Greengage   Plum

1 *Rosa* 'Nevada'

2 *Rosa* 'Fruhlingsgold'

Crab apple   Heritage roses + lilies   Crab appl

2 *Rosa* 'Buff Beauty'

Plum   Plum   Crab apple

1 *Lonicera periclymenum*

1 Jasmine

1 *Lonicera periclymenum* 'Serotina'

1 *Rosa* 'Souvenir o

3 Conference pears

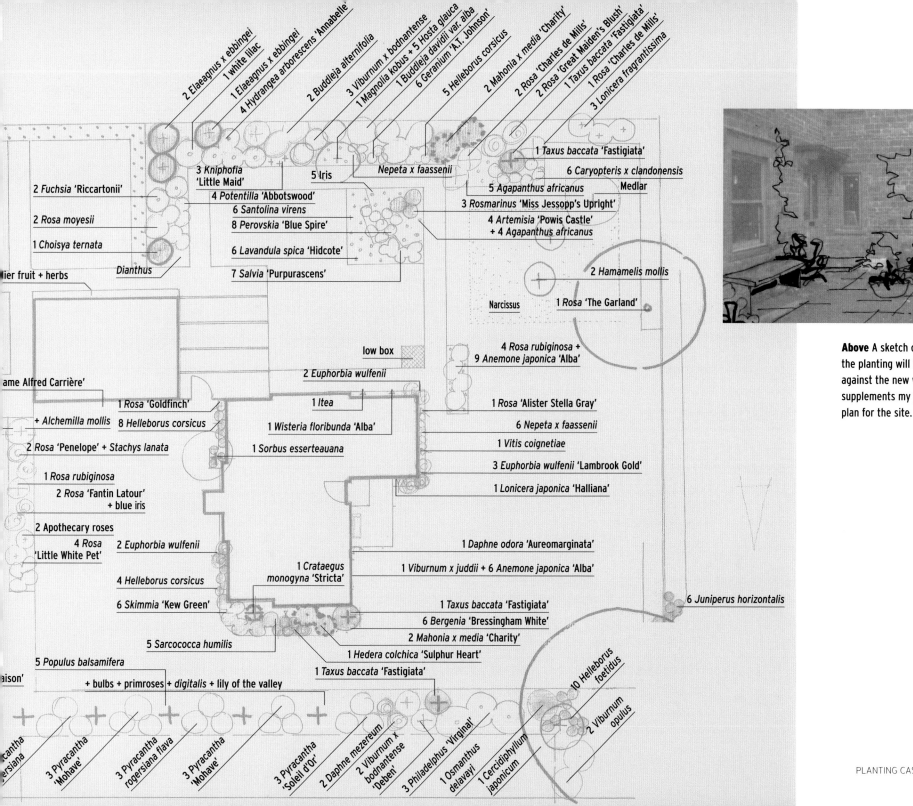

2 Elaeagnus x ebbingei
1 white lilac
1 Elaeagnus x ebbingei
4 Hydrangea arborescens 'Annabelle'
2 Buddleja alternifolia
3 Viburnum x bodnantense
1 Magnolia kobus + 5 Hosta glauca
1 Buddleja davidii var. alba
6 Geranium 'A.T. Johnson'
5 Helleborus corsicus
2 Mahonia x media 'Charity'
2 Rosa 'Charles de Mills'
2 Rosa 'Great Maiden's Blush'
1 Taxus baccata 'Fastigiata'
1 Rosa 'Charles de Mills'
3 Lonicera fragrantissima

1 Taxus baccata 'Fastigiata'

3 Kniphofia
'Little Maid'
5 Iris
Nepeta x faassenii
6 Caryopteris x clandonensis

2 Fuchsia 'Riccartonii'
4 Potentilla 'Abbotswood'
5 Agapanthus africanus
Medlar

2 Rosa moyesii
6 Santolina virens
3 Rosmarinus 'Miss Jessopp's Upright'

8 Perovskia 'Blue Spire'
4 Artemisia 'Powis Castle'
+ 4 Agapanthus africanus

1 Choisya ternata
6 Lavandula spica 'Hidcote'

ier fruit + herbs
7 Salvia 'Purpurascens'

Dianthus
2 Hamamelis mollis

Narcissus
1 Rosa 'The Garland'

low box
4 Rosa rubiginosa +
9 Anemone japonica 'Alba'

2 Euphorbia wulfenii

ame Alfred Carrière'
1 Itea
1 Rosa 'Alister Stella Gray'

1 Rosa 'Goldfinch'
1 Wisteria floribunda 'Alba'
6 Nepeta x faassenii

+ Alchemilla mollis
8 Helleborus corsicus
1 Sorbus esserteauana
1 Vitis coignetiae

2 Rosa 'Penelope' + Stachys lanata
3 Euphorbia wulfenii 'Lambrook Gold'

1 Rosa rubiginosa
1 Lonicera japonica 'Halliana'

2 Rosa 'Fantin Latour'
+ blue iris

2 Apothecary roses

4 Rosa
'Little White Pet'
2 Euphorbia wulfenii
1 Daphne odora 'Aureomarginata'

1 Viburnum x juddii + 6 Anemone japonica 'Alba'

4 Helleborus corsicus
1 Crataegus
monogyna 'Stricta'

6 Skimmia 'Kew Green'
1 Taxus baccata 'Fastigiata'
6 Bergenia 'Bressingham White'

5 Sarcococca humilis
2 Mahonia x media 'Charity'

1 Hedera colchica 'Sulphur Heart'

5 Populus balsamifera
1 Taxus baccata 'Fastigiata'

aison'
+ bulbs + primroses + digitalis + lily of the valley

6 Juniperus horizontalis

10 Helleborus
foetidus

2 Viburnum
opulus

cantha
ersiana
3 Pyracantha
'Mohave'
3 Pyracantha
rogersiana flava
3 Pyracantha
'Mohave'
3 Pyracantha
'Soleil d'Or'
2 Daphne mezereum
2 Viburnum x
bodnantense
'Deben'
3 Philadelphus 'Virginal'
1 Osmanthus
delavayi
1 Cercidiphyllum
japonicum

Above A sketch of how the planting will fill in against the new walls supplements my planting plan for the site.

Planting case study: Wild planting

This next garden is located on mid-Sussex clay. Its owners, who have just moved and who are about to renovate the house, are both very keen gardeners. And it was after seeing my own garden (young designers note!), that they approached my office for advice.

I quoted, visited and was given a very comprehensive brief – but the view was pretty good also, into horse-grazed pastures, and I suggested a ha-ha, so with that and the obvious location for the swimming pool the design took off.

The clients wanted a large vegetable garden, somewhere to plant their collection of boxwoods (a new one on me), Koi pools and a large decorative, though wild pond.

As the ground rises very slightly away from the house – the pond would have to be slightly above the levels of the house. This was something of a worry, both visually and practically, if the thing flooded, but by subtle shaping we evolved a principle whereby all the drainage and overflow from the pond area could be channelled into the ha-ha ditch and away from the lower garden and house.

To link the necessary semi-formal area of boxwood with the wild pond I designed a gravel meander/dry stream which would be planted with increasingly more native plant material as you moved up and away from the house. This way one had less stiff clay soil to modify before planting as they would be growing native material, which can cope.

It was decided to raise the beds with sleepers in the vegetable garden and import good organic topsoil to fill them for maximum production.

To end the ha-ha ditch, and to screen a necessary fence running away from the house I have proposed a low mound, using the ditch and pond excavation, which is to be planted with hazels and birch and establish a ground pattern of wild primroses and early narcissus in spring. This grouping will become the fulcrum around which the garden develops.

Right A new garden plan which combines formality near the house which gradually dissipates into softer planting, a pond and then the countryside beyond.

Above Meandering paths create a restful dynamic, slowing down the pace.

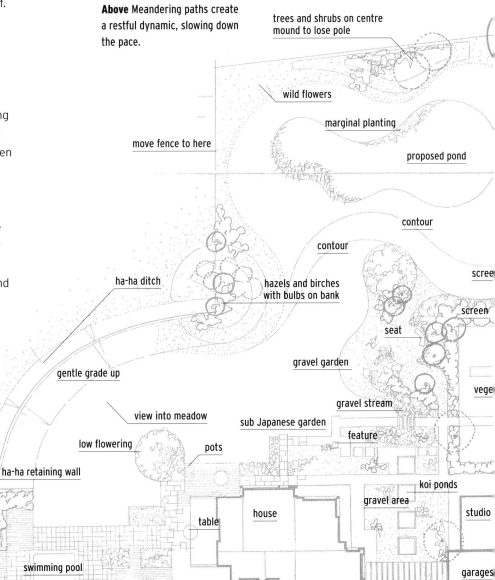

trees and shrubs on centre mound to lose pole

wild flowers

marginal planting

proposed pond

move fence to here

contour

contour

scree

ha-ha ditch

hazels and birches with bulbs on bank

screen

seat

gravel garden

screen

gentle grade up

gravel stream

vege

view into meadow

sub Japanese garden

feature

low flowering

pots

ha-ha retaining wall

koi ponds

gravel area

seat

table

house

studio

swimming pool

garages

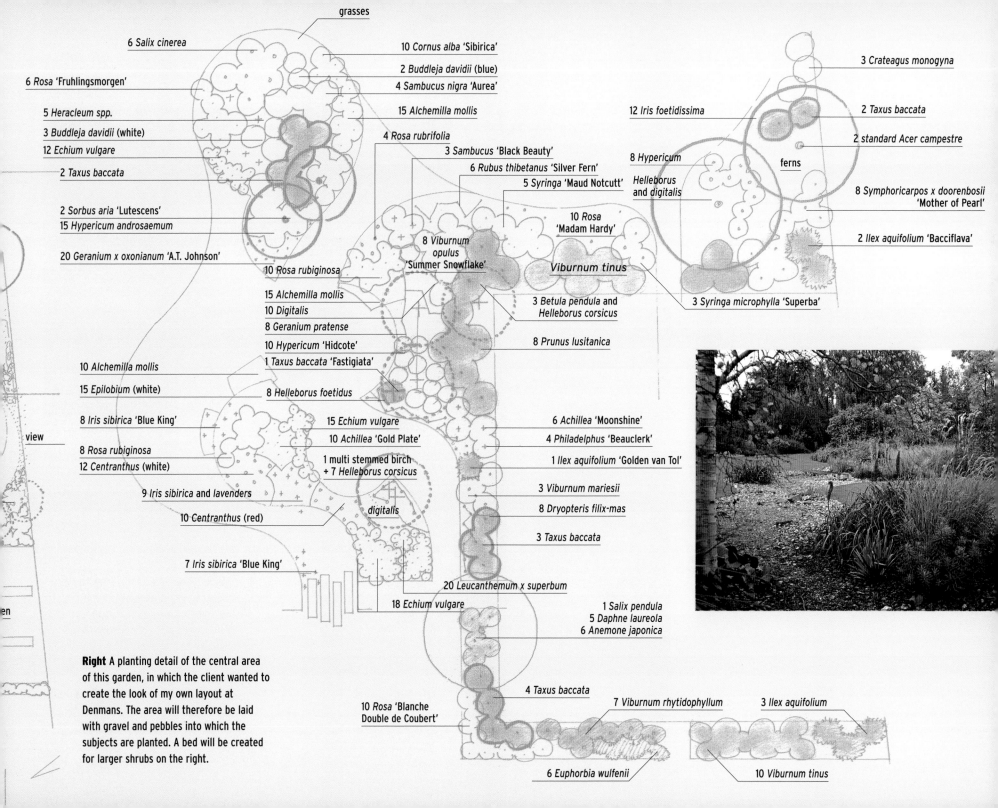

grasses

6 *Salix cinerea*

10 *Cornus alba* 'Sibirica'

2 *Buddleja davidii* (blue)

4 *Sambucus nigra* 'Aurea'

15 *Alchemilla mollis*

3 *Crateagus monogyna*

12 *Iris foetidissima*

2 *Taxus baccata*

2 standard *Acer campestre*

6 *Rosa* 'Fruhlingsmorgen'

5 *Heracleum spp.*

3 *Buddleja davidii* (white)

12 *Echium vulgare*

2 *Taxus baccata*

2 *Sorbus aria* 'Lutescens'

15 *Hypericum androsaemum*

20 *Geranium x oxonianum* 'A.T. Johnson'

4 *Rosa rubrifolia*

3 *Sambucus* 'Black Beauty'

6 *Rubus thibetanus* 'Silver Fern'

5 *Syringa* 'Maud Notcutt'

8 *Hypericum*

Helleborus and *digitalis*

ferns

8 *Symphoricarpos x doorenbosii* 'Mother of Pearl'

2 *Ilex aquifolium* 'Bacciflava'

10 *Rosa* 'Madam Hardy'

8 *Viburnum opulus* 'Summer Snowflake'

Viburnum tinus

10 *Rosa rubiginosa*

15 *Alchemilla mollis*

10 *Digitalis*

8 *Geranium pratense*

10 *Hypericum* 'Hidcote'

1 *Taxus baccata* 'Fastigiata'

8 *Helleborus foetidus*

3 *Betula pendula* and *Helleborus corsicus*

8 *Prunus lusitanica*

3 *Syringa microphylla* 'Superba'

10 *Alchemilla mollis*

15 *Epilobium* (white)

8 *Iris sibirica* 'Blue King'

8 *Rosa rubiginosa*

12 *Centranthus* (white)

9 *Iris sibirica* and *lavenders*

10 *Centranthus* (red)

digitalis

15 *Echium vulgare*

10 *Achillea* 'Gold Plate'

1 multi stemmed birch + 7 *Helleborus corsicus*

6 *Achillea* 'Moonshine'

4 *Philadelphus* 'Beauclerk'

1 *Ilex aquifolium* 'Golden van Tol'

3 *Viburnum mariesii*

8 *Dryopteris filix-mas*

3 *Taxus baccata*

7 *Iris sibirica* 'Blue King'

20 *Leucanthemum x superbum*

18 *Echium vulgare*

1 *Salix pendula*
5 *Daphne laureola*
6 *Anemone japonica*

view

Right A planting detail of the central area of this garden, in which the client wanted to create the look of my own layout at Denmans. The area will therefore be laid with gravel and pebbles into which the subjects are planted. A bed will be created for larger shrubs on the right.

10 *Rosa* 'Blanche Double de Coubert'

4 *Taxus baccata*

7 *Viburnum rhytidophyllum*

3 *Ilex aquifolium*

6 *Euphorbia wulfenii*

10 *Viburnum tinus*

Planting case study: A front garden

This is the front garden of a detached suburban house in southeast England. It is above a main road and had a steep bank down to pavement level, a fairly steep driveway up to the garage and steps to the front door. The front garden is surrounded by large pines, which have become tall, provide no privacy, but whose roots hold the bank. The remainder of the planting is dominated by a group of established cordylines opposite the front door.

The planting, is extremely simple: ground cover of silver/white-leafed *Lamium maculatum*, with a few agapanthus through it, and a fluffy bed of the grass *Deschampsia flexuosa*. Flowery exoticism is introduced near the house with *Plumbago capensis*, which I would plant through with lily flowered tulips, *Daphne odora* for scent, an Irish yew, and some ivy-leafed geraniums to trial in summer. I have supplemented some of the existing shrubs with ground cover: *Cotoneaster horizontalis* and *C. dammeri* under white flowering *Amelanchier canadensis*.

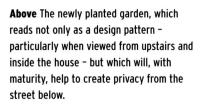

Above The newly planted garden, which reads not only as a design pattern – particularly when viewed from upstairs and inside the house – but which will, with maturity, help to create privacy from the street below.

Left The cut-out concept presented to the client, which I believe is understood far quicker than an outline proposal.

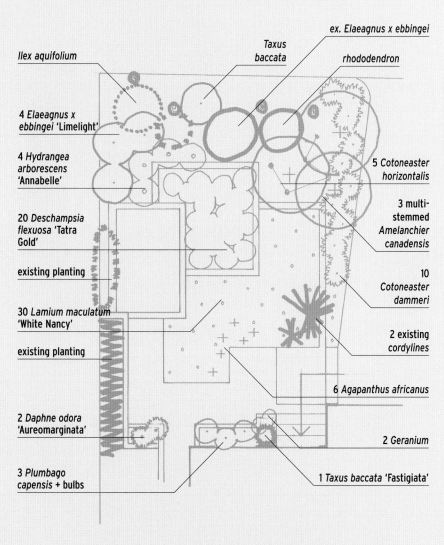

Ilex aquifolium

Taxus baccata

ex. Elaeagnus x ebbingei

rhododendron

4 Elaeagnus x ebbingei 'Limelight'

4 Hydrangea arborescens 'Annabelle'

5 Cotoneaster horizontalis

20 Deschampsia flexuosa 'Tatra Gold'

3 multi-stemmed Amelanchier canadensis

existing planting

10 Cotoneaster dammeri

30 Lamium maculatum 'White Nancy'

existing planting

2 existing cordylines

6 Agapanthus africanus

2 Daphne odora 'Aureomarginata'

2 Geranium

3 Plumbago capensis + bulbs

1 Taxus baccata 'Fastigiata'

Above A planting plan is necessary, however small the site, to see how many plants are needed to fill the space – if nothing else.

Right The completed garden where plants are beginning to infill. I have told the client that he can plant bulbs through any of this material, should he so wish.

5 Specialities

My intention had been to focus on individual aspects of construction in this section, but once you show part of a job, I realised that decisions on detail are never made in isolation, for everything becomes interrelated and it's too irritating to describe what that detail might be - better to show it. It is a visual art we practise after all. And so I end up defining some specialities that have featured in my recent work.

So many decisions, despite the rules I have outlined, are emotional. It's the designer's job to react to the situation, to the house - both inside and out, and most of all to the client. I know that some will add the budget as well, but I feel that that comes later. (After all if you have talked fees and money on the initial contact, the customer must know roughly the bounds within which you work), so it's the design that is important; how that is defined comes later.

Personally my relationship with my client is paramount. I need to agree a wavelength on which to work, and I need to feel trusted. I like to discuss, even argue a point. I really dislike hearing "You're the designer, you know best." I've said before that I want to work with my client, not for them. It makes a huge difference.

To help establish this working relationship, I like to see the interior of the house, difficult if it isn't built, I agree; but I am happy if they come see mine and my garden as well, where possible.

If the garden that I am about to tackle is of any real size I take time to drive around the area before making my approach. This becomes particularly important if you are working abroad and are not familiar with the locality. It's not only to see the local idiom, the plant material, but how their plant material grows as well. See where the wind comes from and generally 'case the joint'. And I find a local nursery or garden

"So many decisions, despite the rules I have outlined, are emotional. It's the designer's reaction to the situation"

centre tells one quite a lot, and certainly gives you an idea of what can and cannot be grown.

Armed with all this plus any landscape history you have picked up along the way, I am ready to look at the site in more detail.

If you are welcomed with "we want a jacuzzi, a swimming pool, a pizza oven, and I hate yellow foliage" - now might be the time to reconsider, and to wish that you had made better initial contact. Be warned. Very, very occasionally you know straightaway that this is not going to work and I would make an excuse and move on. It only gets worse, if you do not, and no one ends up happy.

I thought I would begin by contrasting an inward-looking or closed site with more open ones. And it is this aspect of a job that often defines working in an urban situation as opposed to a rural one, no matter where it is.

Above The designer (me) and entourage on site: the architect, the builder, the client and Martina and Josefina, my associates in South America.

Closed site: Planning for parking

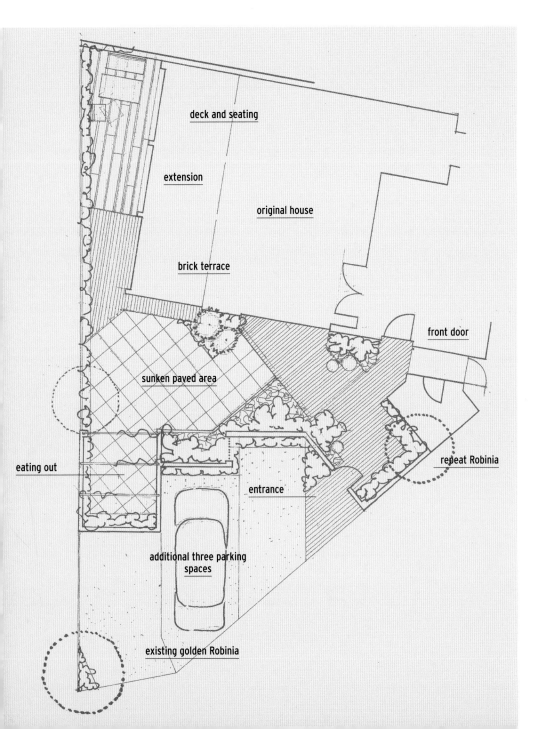

deck and seating

extension

original house

brick terrace

sunken paved area

eating out

entrance

repeat Robinia

additional three parking spaces

existing golden Robinia

front door

This small site could hardly be more inward-looking or closed, and yet because it is near the coast you can smell the sea as soon as you get out of the car and you can hear the screaming seagulls overhead. Some friends have this property as a second home. They have built onto a modest structure to create a huge light and airy general room, where children and grandchildren all meet at weekends for pre- or post-sailing refreshment.

Since the house is within a complex, parking is at a premium, so it was decided to take off the corner of this triangular site to create three extra off-street parking spaces on the outside of a newly built garden wall. The resultant courtyard is fairly miniscule, but allows for front door entry, an eating corner covered by a pergola, and a small afternoon tea corner when sliding windows are drawn back.

Being fully sheltered and facing south, the effect from inside looking out is one of seeing a jungle developing very fast – for we have produced a remarkable suntrap.

Below Provision for cars is a requirement for most of us. A necessity maybe, but there is no reason for not making it attractive.

Opposite Looking down the side of the house you see the zig-zag wall ending in a covered eating recess.

Terraces: First impressions in the US

At one time the main entrance to this North American home was approached via a drive directly in line with the front door, but when vehicles arrived there was insufficient room to turn around, particularly if someone had parked there already. And the client didn't want to spend time looking at parked cars either.

Eventually, parking space was located to the left of the front door, with access for people down some wide granite steps. This utility area was screened by a high wall and cars virtually disappeared.

But what to do with what became a pedestrian area? A pattern was made of limestone (echoing the same stone used to floor the entrance hall) with a coursed granite sett infill between. A secret bench was located in one corner behind a spreading crab apple (*Malus* spp.), looking towards a piece of sculpture.

Flower beds are filled with lavender and creamy Potentilla, with a shrub backing against the wall. To minimise the height of the entrance steps to the house, planters were constructed within the steps, each one containing an Irish yew (*Taxus baccata* 'Fastigiata'). A sweep of wide steps links the courtyard to a grassed lawn.

Above The original entrance provided too small a turning space in front of the house, particularly if several cars were parked together.

Left and right The forecourt becomes a sheltered and decorative paved courtyard. The front door is now approached by granite steps on the left from the new parking area below.

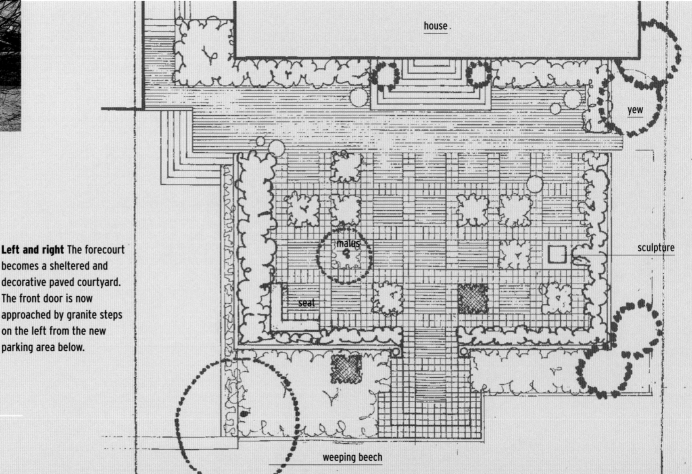

house

yew

malus

sculpture

seat

weeping beech

Right A new flooring pattern was created with granite setts and limestone. Individual beds are filled with lavender and potentilla, and with bulbs in spring.

Above New granite steps lead up from the car park directing the visitor towards the front door.

Left As the planting matures the front entrance becomes less forbidding as the Irish yews (*Taxus baccata* 'Fastigiata') mature, and a better balance is achieved between hard and soft materials.

Construction: English style in the Midwest

I have visited this garden north of Chicago for some years but only really got going when my client decided to remodel her house in the English style.

The frontage had originally had an in-and-out drive. We decided to eliminate one arm of it to create a more intimate copse-like garden beneath large existing trees. There still had to be a parking area, which I patterned using the proportions of the house, to alleviate what was a huge mass of tarmac. Planting is of clipped boxwood on either side of the front door, partly because the shrub is hardy enough to withstand the seasonal temperature swings in this climate zone: snow in winter (and frequent snowfalls can be easily cleared to one side), and fierce heat in summer.

Below the forecourt are woodland walkways underplanted with mysotis, hostas, phlox, ajuga, violas and spring bulbs. In the far corner there is a small pavilion, as both an eye catcher and a useful place to store garden equipment.

The rear garden is dominated by a huge pine tree, which becomes pivotal in terms of the garden plan. Adjacent to the house is a wide sitting room terrace, with columns supporting a pergola frame to be hung with autumn clematis (*Clematis viticella*), which also ramps its way up the neighbouring fir tree.

The main terrace links to another outside the kitchen sliding doors. Here a small pool is located with bird feeders, which provide year-round interest to my clients – and to squirrels, chipmunks and many birds including beautiful cardinals. The principal layout is an oval shape with, to one side, a new rose garden of circular beds in gravel – one colour rose per bed. Behind the rose beds the columns are repeated from the main terrace to create a theatrical backdrop and sitting place to view the garden. The pattern continues round with shrub borders mixed with perennials and shrub roses. Taller tree planting at the rear, screens a neighbouring garden.

Left The grid effect of the bricks in the forecourt echoes the construction of the house itself and pleasingly breaks up what would otherwise be a bland stretch of parking area. I am looking for two 'snooty' dogs in lead to go either side of the front door, though the lamps might have to go.

Opposite The materials used in the walls, steps and edging to the beds unify the garden design. Wide proportions and curves soften any austerity of this otherwise formal house.

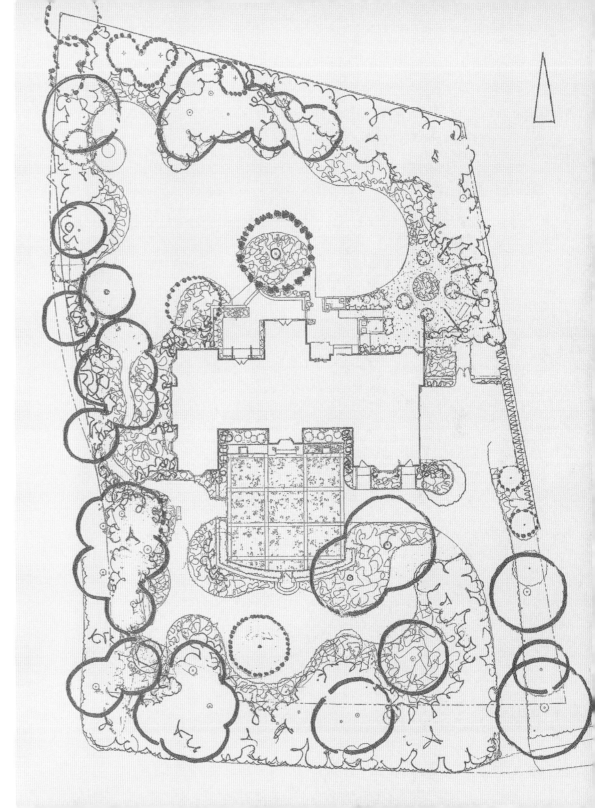

Diagonally across the garden from the circular rose beds is another circular paved terrace, a cool place to sit on hot summer evenings. Mixed shade planting fills the pattern as it returns to the house.

My client is particularly keen on shrub roses, and has a border of them with perennials growing through the gaps along with with big boxwood globes to give some 'oomph' for long winter months. In a comparatively small planting area, shrub roses can quickly get very messy and sprawl, so we have introduced wooden pyramids to contain them and make them more tree-like. They work rather well architecturally with the boxwood globes.

A narrow side piece of garden, leading to the front of the house, is planted in a similar woodland way, with maples, hostas, heuchera with box and yew, under huge oak trees.

Deer are a frequent problem in this area and the front and rear gardens are divided by a high fence on one side of the house with a brick wall and gates on the other.

Left I was surprised to discover years ago just how hot and humid it becomes in the American Midwest in summer. The shade of the huge trees is very welcome and their spreading branches create focal points in the design. Moreover, the dappled effect of light through the foliage effectively breaks up the large expanse of lawn.

Opposite (top left) From below the pergola one looks across lawn. **(Top right)** Woodland planting at the front and to one side of the house. **(Bottom, left and right)** Columns were used on the terrace adjoining the house, and I used most of them to create what I hope will be a rather theatrical semi-circular pergola at the back of a circular rose garden.

Open site: A rural estate

I first visited this very open site professionally in 1990, it is situated in the northeast of England and belongs to a friend from my school days. My client inherited quite a large property but wanted to concentrate his gardening activities on the old walled garden, converting what had been an estate workers cottage into his own weekend home.

The walled garden was large, and on a south-facing slope, so that the house looks over the garden and sheep grazed parkland beyond. In the centre of the top wall of the garden was the old bothy, the gardener's workshop, which on its other side looked into a farmyard.

My job was to design a decorative garden around the house, creating a level lawn or lawns on which to play croquet, with the rest of the site to be planned for growing herbs and vegetables to supply my client's London restaurant. As I remember a local stretch of water yielded excellent freshwater crayfish, and the shoot provided game.

The garden plan was fairly simple: a bold cruciform shape requiring a cut-and-fill exercise to create lawns with sloping banks between them. Being in the northeast (my original home territory) I knew that exoticism was not called for and I revelled in working a known landscape with fairly massive sandstone detailing all round, and a magnificent view beyond.

After 16 years, my client tells me, "All that has happened over the years is seeing the reaction of people to the design. The way the garden flows out into the surrounding parkland, with its endless pastoral effect is what stops them in their tracks. They can spend hours looking at the view, garden and park, not just garden, in the same way as looking out to sea."

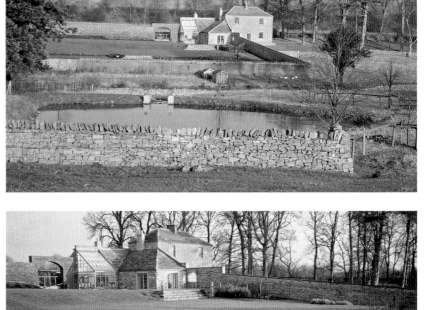

Left Building operations on the conversion of the original cottage, with, on the left, the 'bothy' or gardener's workroom.

Top The newly converted cottage straddles the garden wall, beneath which a stream runs, and here seen from the original parkland on the other side of it.

Above The garden emerges, stepping down from the house terrace. In the lower beds of the south-facing garden herbs will be grown en masse to be taken to London weekly.

"This is especially powerful because the approach is by car and because parking is behind the buildings, on the farmyard side. Now that the surrounding trees have grown, you have no idea of what is waiting for you inside the walled garden until you walk through either house. (The bothy has now been converted for living as well.) So the effect is Wow!, every time."

"They also are captivated by the cedars and Wellingtonias and your design was careful not to spoil this view."

"In order to compete with the setting and view, we have included some bold structures such as the gazebo, statues, pond, 8-foot yew hedging, our own cedar of Lebanon, the garden, we felt, needs this sort of scale to show off your clever use of levels."

A happy client is, for me, the biggest thrill of all!

Main picture and below There is about a 20-year difference between the large picture and the photographs below. The walled garden has matured to create a not- too-demanding foreground to the landscape park beyond. Planting against the bothy wall terminates in a new outside kitchen.

Water: Introduction

Water holds a very significant place in our subconscious, for water is life itself, the magical element that connects all creation at its most basic, and an essential part of the concept of nearly every type of garden in history. And when no water is available we simulate the dry stream bed!

I have never considered myself a particularly watery person and yet, looking back at the gardens I have made, water is a recurring feature - not necessarily for its decorative elements but because I think it allows a space to breathe. It is an open alternative to grass or paving, one that catches the light on even the dullest of days to become the focal point. Used well, a stretch of water is majestic, but all too often we see in gardens bits of water that are far too small, and what I can only describe as being 'diddled up' with false rocks, gnome fishermen and overplanted with too wide a selection of material.

So be bold with the use of water and think through why you want it. Bear in mind that the smaller the area the more difficult it is to look after, and the larger the area the bolder the effect you want to create. But before doing anything, read about the types of water you can introduce into your garden for it will affect the whole layout.

If you are working with water on a large scale, particularly when it has a natural backdrop, make a definite decision as to whether you want your water to look like a man-made design concept, or whether you want to simulate nature. It will affect the shape, the finish (nature does not use concrete or brick edges) and then the planting, which isn't one of this and two of that, but bold swathes of individual species. Will your water be moving or still? If it is near the house, will it be raised for safety, free-standing or on a wall? Do you want to see the water running or spraying, and do you want to hear it trickle or drip?

Whatever type of water feature you settle for, it will inevitably become a focal point for birds throughout the year and bats will dive low across it to drink on summer evenings. Dragonflies will dance over it, and bees will cluster on the lily pads to drink. It can be magical but it can also be dangerous with children around. I urge you to read about water gardening: it's very special and very different.

The following designs will give you a sample of different usages of water in gardens of various sizes.

Right Water looks good, sounds right and can be restful or imposing. It will certainly draw all of God's creatures!

Water: Moving water

Still at the project stage, this garden is being developed around a cottage in the English Midlands. It is a 19th-century property that faces the village street, but at the rear it has a brand-new extension.

Part of the development was to build a pergola – a traditional garden element, but possibly using aluminium for its structure, as a connection with the new. From under the pergola a raised pool, formed like a canal, runs at right angles to it. Halfway down the canal an overflow drops water to a ground level rill – which might be planted in the manner of Lutyens. The rill ends in a step down to another small pool adjacent to the house terrace and from which the water will be pumped back to the canal again.

The idea is that the effect will not only be visual but gently audible as well.

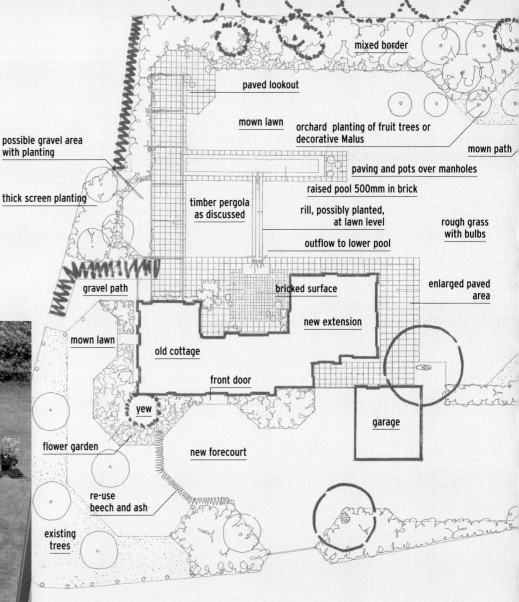

mixed border

paved lookout

mown lawn

orchard planting of fruit trees or decorative Malus

mown path

possible gravel area with planting

paving and pots over manholes

thick screen planting

raised pool 500mm in brick

timber pergola as discussed

rill, possibly planted, at lawn level

rough grass with bulbs

outflow to lower pool

gravel path

bricked surface

enlarged paved area

mown lawn

new extension

old cottage

front door

yew

garage

flower garden

new forecourt

re-use beech and ash

existing trees

Left This is a computer-generated concept of the plan when viewed from upstairs in the house, and gives some idea of what CAD can do.

This lake came about with the need for large amounts of earth to create mounds to screen a proposed road down one side of the site. It is located in the surrounding grassland to a period house and garden, whose tranquillity would be disturbed by traffic noise.

So the lake was excavated, adjacent to a previous 19th-century pond, which had since cracked but remained damp, thereby still making a viable habitat – a marshy plant association – to create a sort of causeway between the old and the new.

The new lake is butyl-rubber lined, with some hard brick edges, and at other places a softer planted edge, allowing access and exit for ducks and other wildlife. There is an island in the pond, with willows as a safe haven from the fox.

The spoil excavated from the lake was used to create a long ridged mound down one side of the property, with minor bumps closer to the lake. Now planted the road is not visible, the noise level is reduced and the irritation of traffic lights at night removed.

Below Water subjects look best planted in bold swathes. In this case I have used the well-known yellow flag iris (*Iris pseudacorus*) with bulrushes (*Typha minima*) beyond.

Above right Looking across the lake to the willow planted island sanctuary. The spoil from the excavation of the lake was used to the right to create screening mounds, which are now planted.

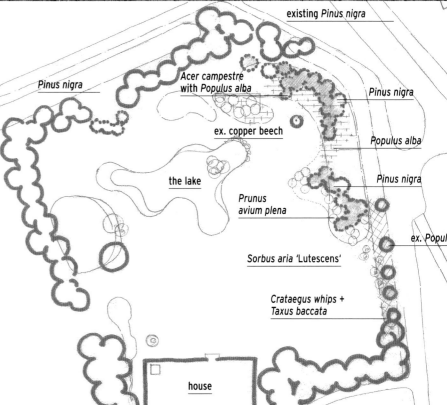

existing *Pinus nigra*

Pinus nigra

Acer campestre with *Populus alba*

Pinus nigra

ex. copper beech

Populus alba

the lake

Pinus nigra

Prunus avium plena

ex. Popul

Sorbus aria 'Lutescens'

Crataegus whips + *Taxus baccata*

house

Water: Tranquil pool

This project I completed in 2005 but my client decided he would like to add the presence of water to his garden. He would lose a bit of his terrace, but gain the advantage of a low wall on which to sit, as he wanted a feature that was raised and still, in which to have water plants and gentle fish.

Built using the same brick as the existing terrace this very simple waterproofed concrete-lined pool was constructed with a brick on edge coping – double thickness on the sitting side. The pool has an outlet and an overflow, and an L-shaped planter for marginals.

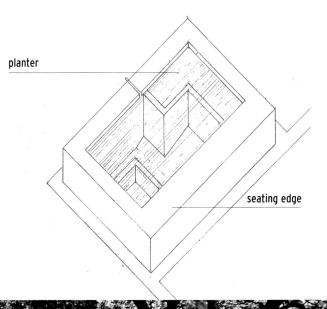

planter

seating edge

Below There is something very attractive about being able to dabble your fingers in water, with lazy fish nibbling them – and it is just this mood that my client wished to create in his brick-paved London garden.

Water: A park in Poland

This is a sort of dream job to which I have been making visits once or twice a year for some time. The house is located a couple of hours by car north of Warsaw. It is a 19th-century Italianate house, in which Chopin is reputed to have played, though after that its career was somewhat chequered with first a German occupation, then a Russian one, before a much-needed restoration by its current Polish residents. The owners are very appreciative of their garden and are therefore ideal clients, though we have to communicate through an interpreter.

The Polishness of the wooded and farmed landscape through which I drive to reach this site, cannot really be expressed in the garden, since the house itself has such period character. The house is approached from the east up a formal drive with a colonnaded façade in white stucco. The south terrace, occupying a hillside site, has views over the garden to a distant lake, with a foreground church. To the west the house looks down a steep incline to its own wooded lake, and to the north is a flat, partly shaded garden and a partly open flower garden.

A German landscape architect had been working there before I was involved and put in steep steps down to the lake on the west side and had also created a shaded perennial garden on the north side which is maturing nicely. What went wrong I have no idea, I am just thankful it did!

I started working on the south side of the house by suggesting a new terrace, which could be approached from the dining room. We had a mock-up made before it was built. This new terrace looked down upon a succession of other levels, with a rose garden over to the left and the silhouette of the village church beyond, and, to the right, a stepping down to the first of three small pavilions and a little secret flower garden. (Currently a covered swimming pool is going in beneath the small pavilion.) Below the main terrace a mask fountain overflows into a large square pool.

Above right The new terrace on the south side of the house, where meals are regularly taken.

Centre right The terrace is a series of terraces stepping down, past an existing group of willows which had to be incorporated. One way leads to the first pavilion and flower garden.

Right The combination of the sight and sound of the running water is soothing and attractive.

the new lake

flower

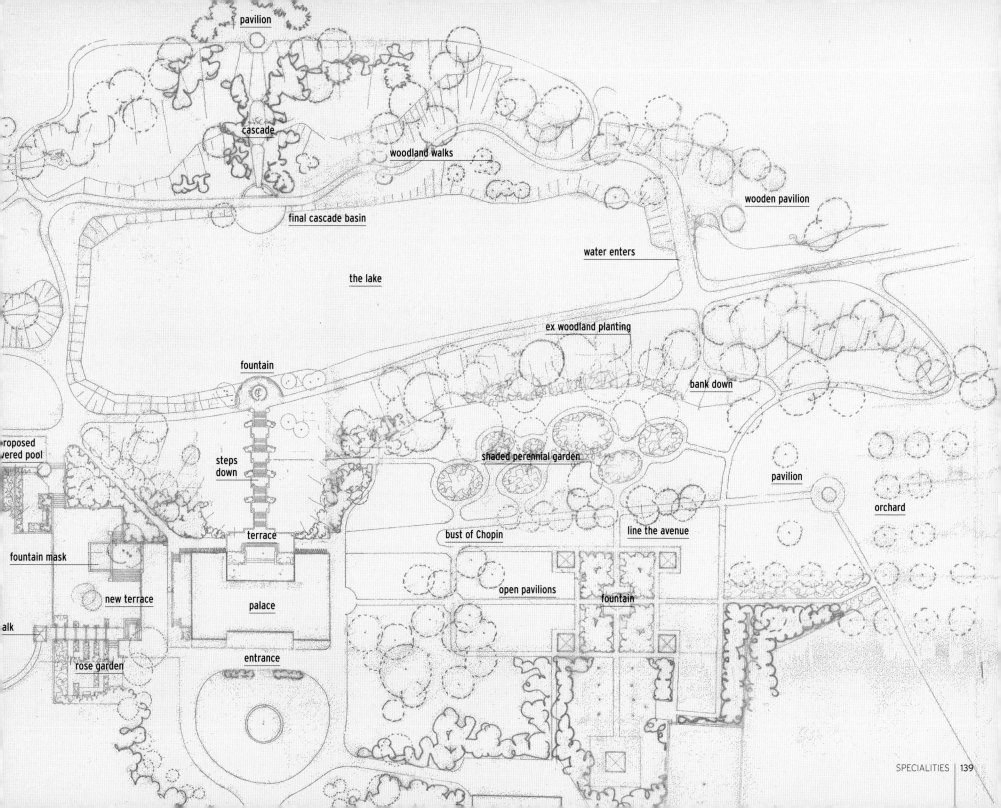

pavilion

cascade

woodland walks

wooden pavilion

final cascade basin

water enters

the lake

ex woodland planting

fountain

bank down

proposed
~~vered~~ pool

shaded perennial garden

pavilion

steps
down

orchard

fountain mask

terrace

bust of Chopin

line the avenue

new terrace

open pavilions

~~alk~~

palace

fountain

rose garden

entrance

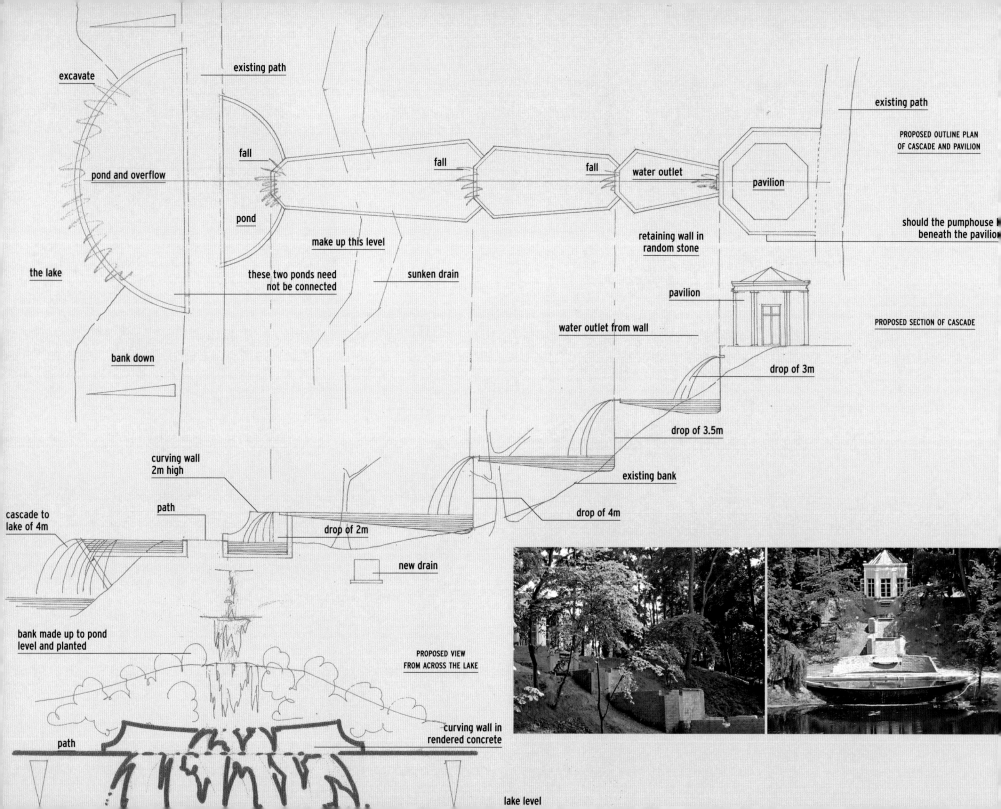

excavate

existing path

existing path

fall

fall

fall

water outlet

pavilion

pond and overflow

pond

should the pumphouse
beneath the pavilion

the lake

make up this level

retaining wall in
random stone

these two ponds need
not be connected

sunken drain

pavilion

PROPOSED SECTION OF CASCADE

water outlet from wall

bank down

drop of 3m

drop of 3.5m

existing bank

curving wall
2m high

path

drop of 4m

cascade to
lake of 4m

drop of 2m

new drain

bank made up to pond
level and planted

PROPOSED VIEW
FROM ACROSS THE LAKE

curving wall in
rendered concrete

path

lake level

The western view from the house down the great flight of steps needed a stop. I first put in a circular pool and fountain at the base of the steps. Then my client, with a rush of blood to the head, wanted a cascade coming down the hill at the other side of the lake. A cascade was a new one on me!

Parallel with the lake ran a deep overflow ditch and this needed to be piped first, so as not to impede the cascade, but then it had to be covered in earth, a minimum of 1 metre deep, so that the grade ran through from the lake to the bank.

We decided to dig another lake in the far southwest corner of the site, and to use the excavated earth to backfill the drain run. It was completed to great effect.

I decided that the cascade should spew out from beneath a second small pavilion located at the top of the hill. The water crashes into four or five basins, goes under the footpath round the lake, and ends in a great saucer which hangs out over the lake.

I could draw exactly what I wanted, and a brilliant engineer and building contractor working for my client were able to construct it all in concrete and stone. Earth had then to be ramped up to the basins and planted with azaleas and rhododendrons (my client's favourites), which are rarely possible in Poland on account of the cold winters, but which are sheltered enough in this location. (We had a late night celebration in the little pavilion at the top of the cascade and a very exciting switch on.)

Left This sequence shows the second pavilion sits at the top of the new cascade running below it. The path becomes a bridge, crossing the lowest level of water before it flows out of a huge saucer into the lake.

Right The foreground fountain is on the house side of the lake at the bottom of a flight of steps.

To the north of the site, surrounding a central flower garden, are four open metal pavilions, which are covered in climbers by the end of the season. I have just had installed a square brick seat in the middle of each pavilion, with a small fountain at the centre. This whole complex ends in the third of my stucco pavilions, and is viewed from the main west terrace at the end of an avenue of lime trees (*Tilia* spp.). This latest pavilion looks into a newly acquired piece of ground, which has been planted as an apple and cherry orchard.

The scale of this private work in Eastern Europe is currently, I believe, quite unprecedented.

Left, above & right I used painted galvanised metal to create a pergola adjacent to the garden near the house, and a further five small pavilions in the flower garden. The raised fountains in their centres provide a seating place on their surrounds. The third pavilion culminates the end of the avenue from the main terrace on the west side of the house.

Restoration: A cathedral close

The whole business of restoration I find quite fascinating for when is one carrying out a makeover and when is one undertaking a restoration job and restoring to what and to when? For a garden is not a finite thing, it continually changes and pure restoration must be back to a recorded time - a detailed description or an old print.

On the other hand, it always seems to me that the marvel of an English town, village, old house or garden is that they have bits tacked on to them throughout their existence - and each bit is hopefully of its period - so where does this leave restoration? The secret, I believe, is to develop with sensitivity towards the past, but not let it overwhelm the present.

This particular restoration project is within a medieval cathedral close in a city in the west of England. The house is historic, with Victorian and early 20th-century alterations, and is currently undergoing considerable updating. The large garden is long and thin running down to the river. Gertrude Jekyll is reputed to have said when visiting that the garden had some of the finest and longest herbaceous borders that she had seen within it. These borders are totally overgrown with weed, which is something of a burden to overcome, particularly now that only limited maintenance possible.

More importantly for the present owners is the progression from the rear of the house into the first part of the garden - currently a rather moth-eaten pattern of box-edged beds - all enclosed from the rest of the garden by a thick yew hedge.

I propose making a huge hole in the hedge to open up the space and to remove a good proportion of the box patterned beds. This way, it is possible to create a viable paved courtyard readily accessible to the house. (Presumably, accessibility was never a priority prior to the latter half of the 20th century - tea was taken on the lawn, and it was all carried by maids for miles!)

Once opened up the central axis runs down the second section of the garden, but does not centre on double gates which lead into the Jekyll borders. Further more, on the site of a previous derelict summerhouse, a new pavilion is called for tucked round the corner, and facing due south. This, I suspect, will become the main gathering point in the garden for visiting grandchildren and summer parties.

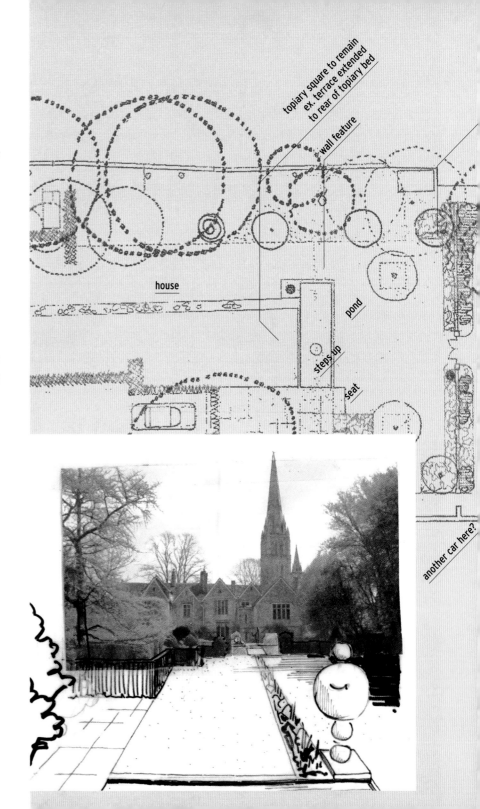

topiary square to remain
ex. terrace extended to rear of topiary bed
wall feature
house
pond
steps up
seat
another car here?

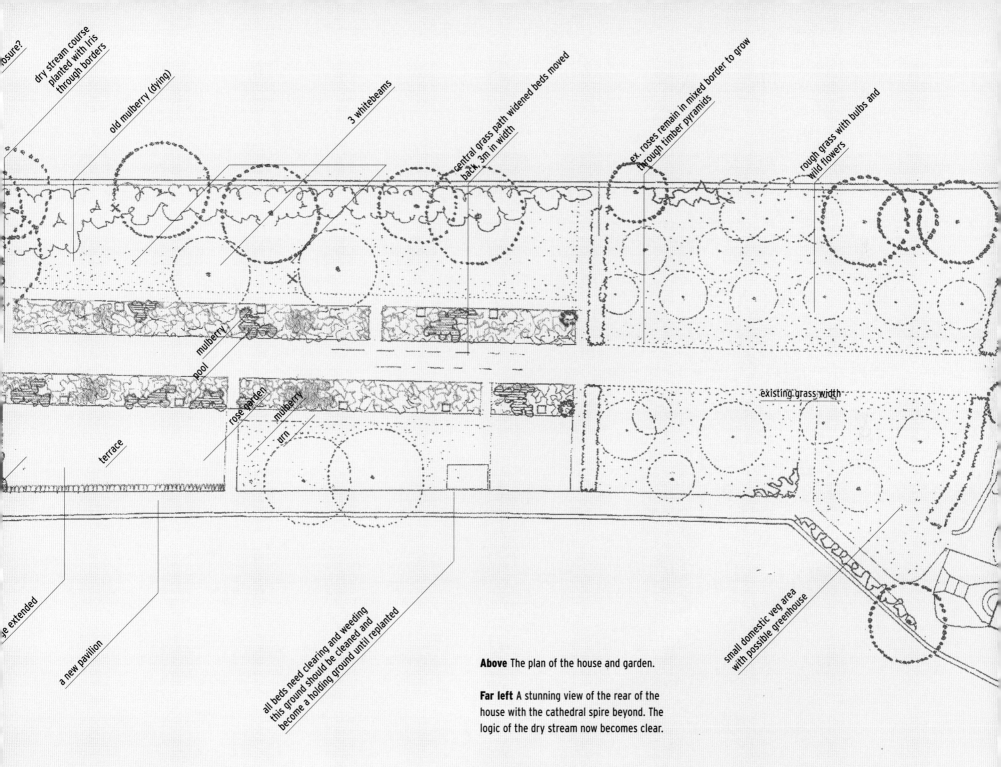

dry stream course
planted with iris
through borders

osure?

old mulberry (dying)

3 whitebeams

central grass path widened beds moved
back, 3m in width

ex. roses remain in mixed border to grow
through timber pyramids

rough grass with bulbs and
wild flowers

mulberry)

pool

rose garden

mulberry

urn

terrace

existing grass width

ge extended

a new pavilion

all beds need clearing and weeding
this ground should be cleaned and
become a holding ground until replanted

small domestic veg area
with possible greenhouse

Above The plan of the house and garden.

Far left A stunning view of the rear of the
house with the cathedral spire beyond. The
logic of the dry stream now becomes clear.

Left and below left I used two Spanish urns and a pool to try to visually reconcile the fact that the gate to the borders is not in line with the centre of the garden. The existing pool will move away from the gate and when rebuilt will be much cleaner in outline and planting.

A lily pool running at a 90-degree angle to the pavilion becomes the fulcrum of the garden and the turning point for the main axis to move over. Two large Spanish urns help this movement, one at the end of the pond and the other to the right of the gate into the next garden.

It is from this central point of the garden looking back towards the house that I think you get a very fine view of it with the spire of Salisbury cathedral beyond. The height of the spire can be replicated in a dry rill which runs from a pool in the first courtyard to the lily pool. Currently many of the beds in the garden have random stone edging, which on inspection is carved stone. I propose using these carved stones for my dry rill.

There are now three further sections of the garden. Through the iron gates the Jekyll borders, which are being cleaned currently, everything in them is being lifted and stored in a nursery area to really get to grips with the weed. The central grass path can be widened, and the borders on either side likewise. Collapsing vertical posts and chains for roses are being replaced by stout obelisks to provide support. Eventually the borders will be replenished with more woody material to provide both winter interest and a strong skeleton to support the perennial planting.

There is a box division between this section and the next, which had a pair of perennial borders, too. These, I think, should be eliminated and this part of the garden could become an orchard, with in spring bulbs growing in rough grass. Finally beyond high yew hedges you come to a narrow strip of grass which fronts onto a swift-moving, chalk stream, with water meadows beyond. This final garden is dominated by a charming 18th-century lookout, approached up steps. This was where one made one's excursion for afternoon tea I suppose.

Of course maintenance becomes a very big word in the redevelopment of such a garden, and only two very keen gardeners would dream of taking on such a project. I hope that they will be rewarded by the result.

Below The view through the iron gates down the central axis to the borders about which Miss Jekyll wrote.

Right The garden to this property has been recorded since the 18th century, so one treads warily.

Restoration: A sunken garden

This is what I would describe as a Bertie Wooster sort of house above the Thames valley in Berkshire. The current owners, for whom I had worked before, have saved this building from public usage, to make it into a very comfortable private home again.

There was the usual clearance required at the front of the house of overgrown shrubbage - though allowing a certain amount of rusticity to create atmosphere and, more importantly, to provide discreet parking and a service entrance.

The real excitement came at the side of the house, where a sunken garden adjoined a marvellous Edwardian conservatory. But sunken gardens are devils: unless well-built the retaining walls usually leak, and there is not enough either topsoil or drainage left at the lower sunken level. A sad-looking rose garden was the norm.

Such a garden needs to be full and romantic. The main terrace looks out onto a lawn with cedars and topiary and, in the distance, a glimpse of the snaking River Thames.

We decided to clear out the space, do repairs and plant up the sunken area in a squared pattern, though abstracting the planting, so that everything didn't balance with everything else. The dark green of box and yew mix with grey santolina and purple sage.

From the sunken area a terrace and gravel paths lead round the house to a stone-balustraded dining terrace. The house screamed out for evergreen choisya masses (not Aucuba), for palm trees (Chaemerops, the hardiest), with masses of lilies in pots and geraniums in summer. The terrace was edged with a balustrading to match that surrounding the roof of the house and through it 'Dorothy Perkins' roses and clematis ramble.

It is very cheering that such a property can be given a new life.

Right The plan of the sunken garden which was planted with roses and a badly drained lawn. Now restyled with evergreen and evergrey plant material it provides interest from the conservatory all the year round. The ultimate differing heights of vegetation relate to the evergreen planting which surrounds the sunken area.

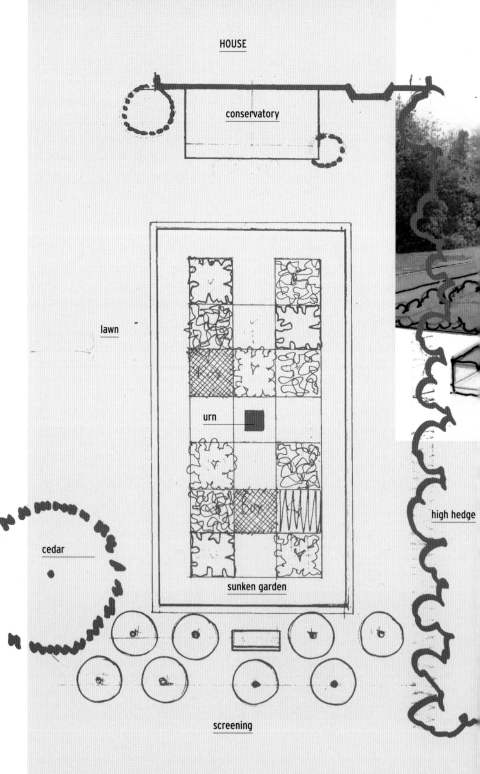

"It is very cheering that such a property can be given a new life."

Closed site: Re-creation

I think it important that restoration work should not only be of large gardens, but small ones as well. I suspect we are letting some important 20th-century gardens slip through the restoration net, because no one has seen them other than their owner.

For this reason I wanted to include this garden design exhibited at the 2006 Chelsea Flower Show. Inspiration for the layout was drawn from a study of the modernist architecture of Farnsworth House, built between 1946 and 1950, by Mies van der Rohe. The first demonstration of Mies van der Rohe's individual manner was the German pavilion at the 1929 Barcelona Exhibition, which became a prototype for modernist architects. It was the bold, geometric approach of the design of Farnsworth House that inspired designers Marcus Barnett and Phillip Nixon to create this project. The link between architecture and planting is articulated by the geometric shapes of tightly clipped box (*Buxus sempervirens*). The remaining planting softens the overall geometry and introduces colour, foliage and texture. The trees provide dappled shade and movement as well as height. At the rear of the garden is a loggia, a point of destination and a peaceful space from which to admire the garden.

Opposite, above and left The essential geometry of the design is emphasised by elements such as the path, the water, and the vertical ranks of wood and light boxes on the wall, all softened by the planting. The view from the loggia, at the rear of the garden, highlights the different elements and shapes, emphasising the importance of context and contrast in the design.

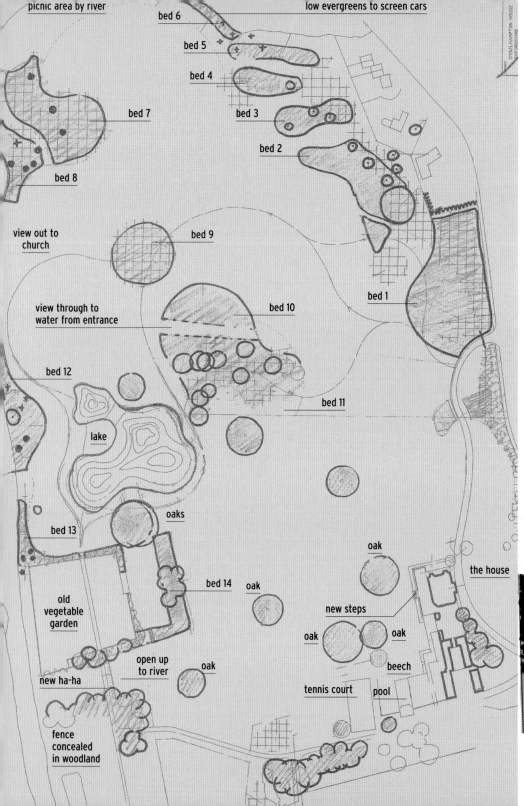

picnic area by river

low evergreens to screen cars

bed 6

bed 5

bed 4

bed 3

bed 7

bed 2

bed 8

view out to church

bed 9

bed 1

view through to water from entrance

bed 10

bed 12

bed 11

lake

oaks

bed 13

oak

the house

bed 14

oak

old vegetable garden

new steps

oak

oak

open up to river

oak

beech

new ha-ha

tennis court

pool

fence concealed in woodland

Open site: The grand scale

This manor house in the Midlands of England dates from 1768. It is therefore a listed building, and any work on the house and its surroundings had to be approved by the appropriate authorities. This was not restoration exactly, rather development in sympathy with what exists.

At one time the house was visible from the road, and I had always thought that it appeared too tall upon its site, but its current owners screened my view with planting some years ago.

The house is accompanied by outbuildings, a very fine Regency conservatory, a swimming pool and at one time two enormous conifers, *Taxodium distichum*, which dominated both the pool and conservatory. Exploration by a tree surgeon happily discovered that both trees were no longer safe and they were felled, opening up the garden enormously.

My clients, who have a large, young family, were open to suggestions, though everything had to be user-friendly, and scaled for entertaining. A flower garden was required, and a remodelling of the terrace around the

Left A view of the estate with proposed planting masses, the lake and their relationship to the house and garden.

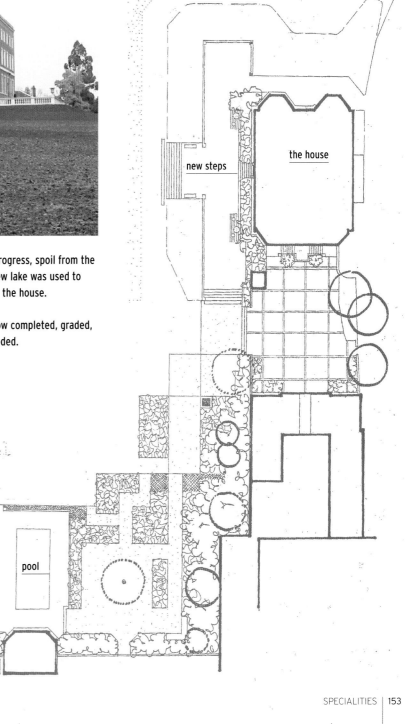

house. The site needed much tree planting to organize the views and generally give the surrounding oak-studded grassland an upgrade, for there are fine views from the house.

The house was surrounded on two sides by a collapsing brick walled ha-ha, and a major decision was to eliminate this rather than rebuild it – the idea being that the house would sit within its grounds and not across from them. When and if the grassland needed grazing a temporary electric fence could be erected.

My first task was to visually lower the house on its south side from the approach drive. By proposing a 1.5-metre (5-feet) high retaining wall along the south side of the house and grading up to it, we could lose half a storey, and as the wall was 3 metres (10 feet) from the house light still got into thesub-basement area, which in fact was the children's playroom. This was then joined by a new balustrade to the main terrace, which was to be resurfaced, with new wide steps leading from it.

Left An early proposal for raising a bank to mask the south end of the house which appeared too proud of its landscape. This runs into a proposed new terrace with balustrading.

Above left Work in progress, spoil from the excavations of the new lake was used to create banking round the house.

Above The bank is now completed, graded, and waiting to be seeded.

the house

new steps

tennis court

pool

Once my clients had approved my proposals they were put to their architect who translated them into working drawings necessary for approval by the authorities, pricing and finally building. I would thank the architect for his tact, and very thorough expertise.

A courtyard at the north side of the house, used by the children for ball games, was also brought into the scheme for resurfacing.

During the time it took to have the drawings prepared and go through other procedures, we started to think about the flower garden, swimming pool surround and conservatory. My clients had restored the conservatory, which faces a blue covered swimming pool, to its pristine former self. The pool we needed to hide from the house. So previous banks were replaced by a low retaining wall, which doubled as seating, and a squared flower garden was laid out between the walls and the house, with gravel pathways between. The flower garden was planted up the newer way with mixed perennials and

grasses. I used a lot of blue, yellow and grey-coloured flowers and foliage to work with the swimming pool and its cover. The garden was punctuated with urns, which I re-used, to refer back to the period of the house. In a single year this garden grew enormously well. It is not irrigated, but the ground was well prepared by the contractor, who has been extremely supportive and very patient throughout.

Although the lower part of the ground surrounding this house was bordered by a river, it was within deep banks and could not be seen from the

Below The flower garden complex runs on from the terracing which surrounds the house. A new courtyard was created between it and the old stable block as well. The flower garden surrounds an existing pool, which is looked onto by a fine conservatory.

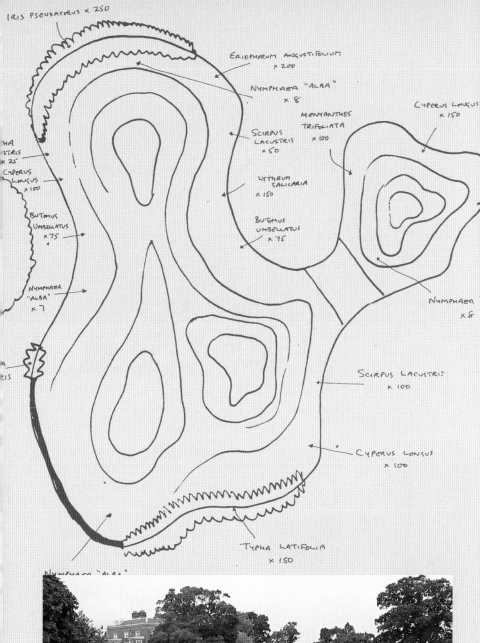

IRIS PSEUDACORUS x 250

ERIOPHORUM ANGUSTIFOLIUM x 200

NYMPHAEA "ALBA" x 8

CYPERUS LONGUS x 150

MENYANTHES TRIFOLIATA x 100

SCIRPUS LACUSTRIS x 50

...THA ...STRIS x 25

CYPERUS LONGUS x 100

LYTHRUM SALICARIA x 150

BUTOMUS UMBELLATUS x 75

BUTOMUS UMBELLATUS x 75

NYMPHAEA "ALBA" x 8

NYMPHAEA "ALBA" x 7

...RIS

SCIRPUS LACUSTRIS x 100

CYPERUS LONGUS x 100

NYMPHAEA "ALBA"

TYPHA LATIFOLIA x 150

Left A sketch to show contouring in the lake. Although I designed the lake outline, a water expert, Martin Kelly, completed the job.

Below The view from the lake area back up the hill to the house.

Above The completed lake, nestling between giant oak trees at the bottom of the hill. From inside the house the view to the lake is uninterrupted by the new retaining wall on the bank around the house.

house. I therefore suggested a lake, above the river, though at the lowest point of the grounds, and which we ultimately discovered could be fed by existing ponds and a watercourse running down the hill to it.

Along the way we discovered where there had been an original house with outbuildings, which called the job to a halt from time to time for further inspection. We had hoped to hit clay on digging for the lake, but after seeking advice from a water expert the pool was lined with butyl rubber over on sand. The butyl rubber is laid over a timber frame all round the pool to create a rigid edging.

Two winters ago the first job I did was to plant up the surrounding grassland to both supplement existing trees and to hide lights from a distant road and neighbouring properties. These plantings are beginning to frame this ambitious concept.

I would like to thank my clients for the pleasure of working with them. This sort of relationship can be very strained but (so far as I am aware) to date has been exemplary.

Vernacular: Patagonia

For some years I have been involved with a garden design school outside Buenos Aires in Argentina. I was asked first to start the school in Santiago, Chile, but found its population too small. Instead, two ex-students from Kew, Martina Casares and Josefina Barzi, decided to take it on and run it from home in Buenos Aires.

The result is that I visit South America once or twice a year and have therefore got one or two jobs as well. My latest, nearly completed, is in the south of Argentina: in Patagonia, in the foothills of the Andes, this bit just like Switzerland - skiing in winter and cool in the summer, so lots of timber-built and wooden-clad houses. Far, very far from wooden shack imagery, and as they are traditionally combined with local stone, the houses look, and are, very robust.

When I first visited the site with my clients, it was steeply wooded with *Nothofagus dombeyii*, the southern beech (or *quoiwe*, as the locals call it) which were enormous. The house was to face a lake with the Andes to be seen on a clear day, and on the other side more mountains. The site rolled down to a wetland on this side.

Above This is the view across the lake from the house location. On a clear day ridges of the Andes are visible beyond those shown.

Far left At the front of the house there is a new drive approach around a damp scrub - at the lower end of which we have created a lake, held by a concrete dam. A bridge on the left crosses this, and the drive comes up the hill to the house.

Left The site being cleared of its timber to allow a clearer view of the lake. The soil is rich, dark and volcanic.

Opposite Pegging out the house position.

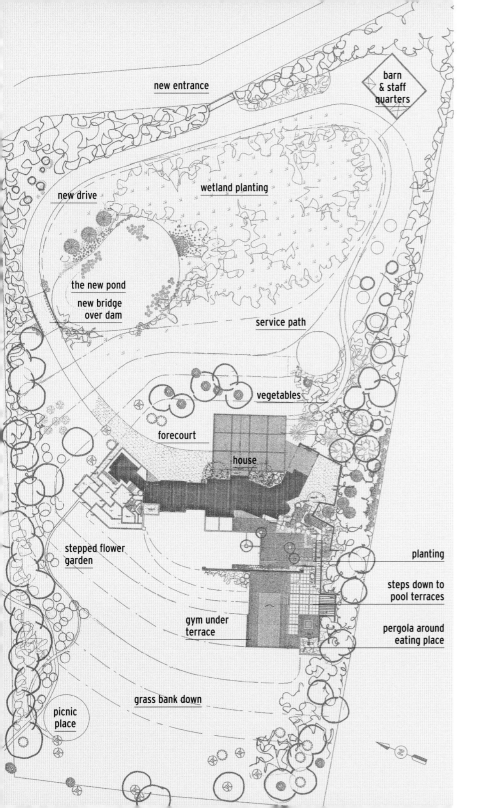

new entrance

barn
& staff
quarters

new drive

wetland planting

the new pond

new bridge
over dam

service path

vegetables

forecourt

house

stepped flower
garden

planting

steps down to
pool terraces

gym under
terrace

pergola around
eating place

grass bank down

picnic
place

The site had to be more or less clear felled – since those trees were of a size that become dangerous as the wind gets into them and blows them down. We then cut into the hillside to create a level platform for the proposed house which had to face both ways. The earth is black, crumbly and volcanic. With a very long-suffering local architect, Ignacio Benavidez, we visited various houses in the vicinity – some quite old – to decide on the form of the house. I was very privileged to be in on these creative decisions.

Eventually plans were drawn up and a model made. The house appears to be two-storey on its approach side but it is in fact three-storey on the side of the lake to accommodate a gym beneath, with a swimming pool beyond. And it had to be an infinity pool – very fashionable here in Patagonia, as elsewhere!

My job was to integrate the levels and design a layout for my client's young family, as well as pretty large spaces for entertaining – barbecues, firepits, the lot. The house needed a new approach drive, which was sited round the wetland (half of which was cleared and flooded) so that as you cross the end of the newly created lake, rumbling over a timber bridge (which conceals a dam),

Right When researching the house type and garden we looked at older traditional wooden houses (above). Elements of this have been included in the new house, beneath which there is a gymnasium and swimming pool on the right. The stone is all granite.

you see the new house on the hill above. You enter the house and through the main rooms is a view of the lake and the Andes beyond. Wow!

My brief was to be as 'of the place' as possible. So I used timber to define the pattern of the main forecourt with a small stone infill, reversing the pattern to be of stone with a timber infill for the main entertaining terrace. We found some lovely old apple trees to shade this terrace which instantly gave character.

Steps lead down to the sheltered swimming pool terrace, which is timber, though a small entrance area is paved to provide an eating alcove and surround to a paddling pool.

All the walls are faced in granite, which now needs planting to soften it all.

I am using as much native planting material as I know - araucaria (monkey puzzles), nothofagus, drimys, eucryphia, azara and fuchsias. The roadsides in spring are yellow with Spanish broom (*Spartium junceum*), and there are

masses of blue lupins everywhere followed by alstroemeria which are sold in bunches at the side of the road. Spruce and larch are common, and of course there is much foreign plant material as well. We have created a small flower garden at the north end of the house which steps down to a path into the ravine. This area is overlooked by a loggia on the garden side of the house and by a playroom.

The newly created lake meets another stream on one side of the site forming a ravine before running into the lake. We have cleared out some of this area prior to planting in the shade a native woodland garden with spring bulbs.

This job has been a wonderful experience of working in another culture with completely foreign material. I have been ably assisted by Martina and Josefina whom I would thank, along with Ignacio the architect who has been very patient with me!

Right The vernacular materials for houses in this high-altitude part of Argentina are timber and granite. The buildings look and are solid and insulating against the mountain temperatures.

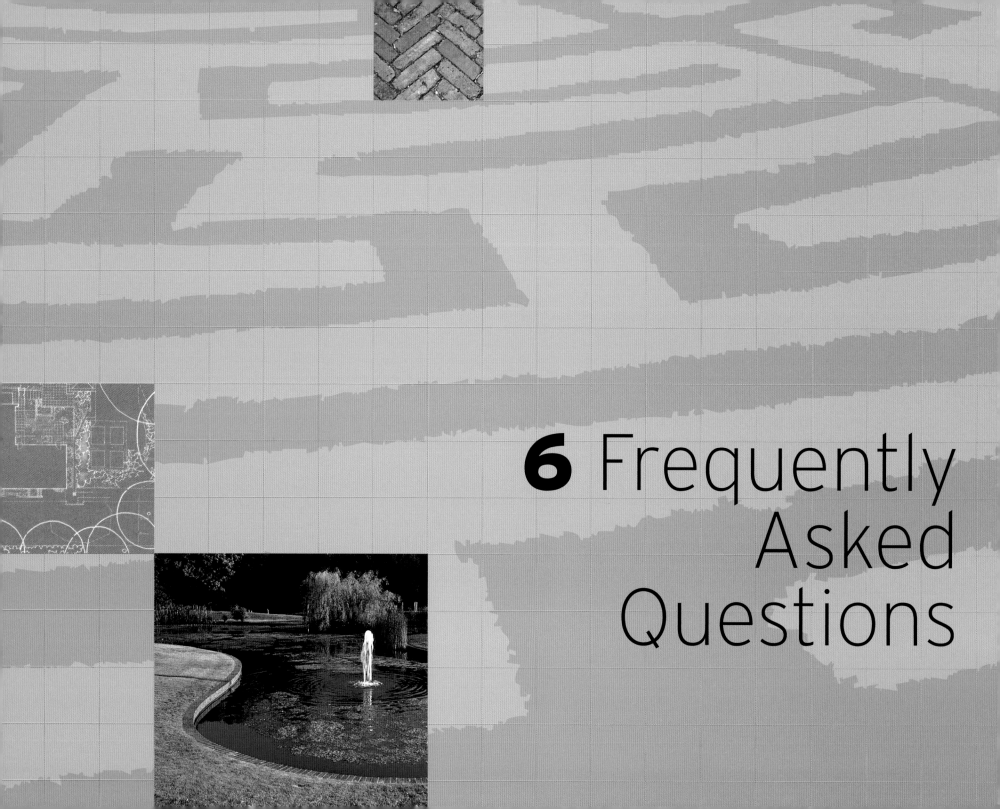

6 Frequently Asked Questions

F requently I am asked to talk to students, which I am happy to do. I well remember good landscape architects and designers like Geoffrey Jellicoe and Russell Page who were terribly helpful when I was starting. (I took Battersea Festival Gardens for my landscape thesis and Russell Page actually met me and showed me around.) Then I worked for Brenda Colvin from whom I learnt a great deal, and later Dame Sylvia Crowe who was a wonderful example, so yes, I am happy to help newcomers, just as I was helped.

BUT, I have no secret formula, just a lot of work, travel and client experience. I sometimes feel that students think if they could just press the correct button I could reveal all. The nice thing is that one is just as challenged by each new situation, as I was when I started. Or so I think.

Garden design is a lonely occupation, which suits me, but it does not, of course, suit everyone. And when you are on your own, only you can resolve the problem, which is why I tell students to sit down on site and establish the sort of design they want there and then. Inspiration

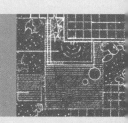

"...I have no secret formula, just a lot of work, travel and client experience."

should come from looking at a site - not looking at a drawing board or even a screen afterwards; that is the place to refine your ideas and make them work to scale.

Photograph and draw on site; I find it helps fix the site in mind. Measuring up all the details does that too - and get something down design wise as soon as possible.

When you go to a new site remember that you have been asked there for your ideas. So start sparking straight away: that is what the client is paying for. For those that don't charge for their first visit, I can only say that often I find it to be the most exciting one and it is when I have most ideas; it should be the most expensive visit in reality!

Which brings one to the dreaded money thing. It is a business, after all, we are running and ideally it should be run like one. So have a set rate. If you are a member of an organisation, they will advise along with your accountant, but it has to do with experience as well. You must get the money business down in writing or in a printed brochure to your client before you do anything else and after the very first contact. At each stage of a job, tell them how much the next phase will be - do it, and get the money in hand before the phase after. The nicest people can develop fangs when money is mentioned. And there are of course plenty of permutations on fee structure, for drawings, advice, visits, travel and other expenses.

1 What are your feelings about restoration of historical gardens?

John Brookes replies:

Restoring to when exactly? My feeling is that a redesign or modification of an old garden should be completed sympathetically to the original – using the same materials – pavings or plantings – but done in a current idiom, all subject to maintenance capabilities of course. Many old gardens had dozens of gardeners and that level of maintenance is just no longer feasible.

Left This 19th-century building has been converted from a retirement home to a private dwelling. It was originally quite a large country house and the layout needed to be expansive, with a permanent planting in an original sunken garden which was bedded out. I wanted to create a sort of Victorian feel with planting against the house of palms and all those sub-tropical plants, which they loved.

Left and below This is the restoration of a garden to an old Sussex manor house. The building suggested a late 17th-century formal approach, so there are two stretches of water which step down to a newly constructed pavilion (below left). To the side of the water is a formal garden beneath the top lawn. All was constructed around large existing masses of yew cut into simple shapes (below).

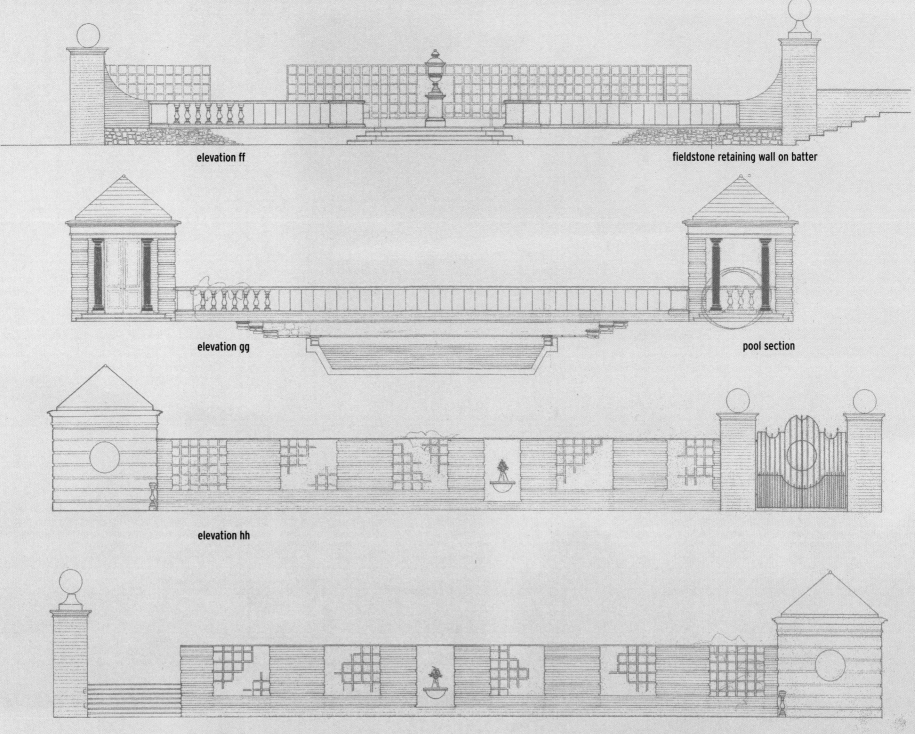

elevation ff

fieldstone retaining wall on batter

elevation gg

pool section

elevation hh

elevation ii

2 Do you need architectural experience? How do you detail structures?

John Brookes replies:

I am not an architect, but it is jolly useful to have a friend who is! What I do is to draw up what I want a building to look like and then get help - an architect sometimes or a site engineer. Structures such as pergolas I think garden designers ought to be able to design. And water features as well. But if in doubt seek help: there is no shame in not knowing, and someone who does know is all too happy to help. When I was starting out I was working in central London a lot in association with Clifton Nurseries as the contractors who built my garden and Victor Shanley, who was in charge of the landscape section, was terribly helpful - a fact I am glad to acknowledge.

Over time of course you see how things are built, and heaven knows there are enough books about (to which I've added a few) to help. Inspiration comes from the flower show gardens I think, and just learning to look and note.

Pergolas are not easy - they can become all too massive, or too flimsy. The secret I think is to decide what the structure is there for and what you want to grow over it. Vines both look heavy and weigh heavy so you do need strength. Well-trained roses and clematis need less bulk in their support.

Opposite These are the constructional details for parts of the English Walled Garden that I designed for the Chicago Botanic Gardens a few years ago. I had never done anything quite so complicated, but luckily I had the help of an architect friend, the late Freddie Fielden, for such elements as roof joists and guttering.

Right The garden is maturing, and the buildings are still standing! The sunken pool owes its ancestry to one at Great Dixter, the late Christopher Lloyd's garden in East Sussex. (**Inset**) The walls were softened with lattice, as it is so difficult in the Midwest climate to achieve this with evergreen climbers.

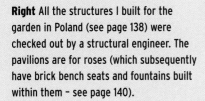

Right All the structures I built for the garden in Poland (see page 138) were checked out by a structural engineer. The pavilions are for roses (which subsequently have brick bench seats and fountains built within them – see page 140).

Right Before building the terrace on the south side of the house, my client had his staff mock up the structures in hardboard, which was very helpful. (**Inset**) The walls became higher so that they could be sat upon instead of including a handrail, and the steps were screened.

Above I planned a pavilion with a fine view in a garden in the US and the client agreed to a hardboard model of it, to see whether he liked the effect. Happily he did. The columns have now been replaced by carved granite.

3 The materials for building a terrace seem limited, particularly if you want more of a well-matured country look and not a hard glaring finish. What do you suggest, and how does one mellow a job quickly?

John Brookes replies:

Building materials vary enormously, and availability is often limited in some parts of the world. So make a collection of available pavings (and their prices) and lay them by your house (if the proposed terrace abuts it), or in a more rural situation lay the collection on grass to be viewed against another structure or soil colour, even foliage colour. And see what the colour is like when the paving is wet too.

The options are stone, reconstituted stone (which is crushed stone mixed again with mortar), concrete, terracotta, slate, granite sett, cobble (rounded and difficult to walk on) or brick. Then there are wood surfaces, or various gravels, even timber mulches.

You can probably eliminate many of these as not being appropriate, not available or too expensive.

And remember you can mix materials as well: brick with stone, granite with slate - it depends what you like and the look you require.

Weathering naturally takes place fairly quickly, and the more textured the hard surface, the better I think the surface looks.

Below The options for paved areas vary in suitability and style, some formal, some informal. Bricks lend themselves to being laid in a repeating pattern. Paving (limestone or concrete slabs) can be random.

Left I enjoy mixing materials, though I try not to make the flooring too 'busy'. Here cedar timber is used as decking, steps and seating between raised timber planters in an Oregon garden.

Above left Limestone tile and granite setts and (**Above**) Granite setts used with Old York stone in an English herb garden. Texturally, the materials are the same, and it works.

4 While I understand your argument for a garden to be 'of its place', how do I achieve the look?

John Brookes replies:

Suppose I start at the negative end; you can probably say what would not be the correct hard material to use for paths and terrace for instance, which brings your options down. So what then is the correct material for your area? Traditionally did they build in timber, brick, flint, adobe, or stone? Were walls rendered, was a traditional colour used, what is the capping to walls? Alternatively, if there are no structures about, what of fences, what type of wood, and are they one-, two- or three-bar, or iron, and also the gates, what were they like?

Now consider your soil – sand, clay, chalk, rich alluvial, bog – and look at the range of plants that grows naturally upon it. Do the plants typically grow

Opposite The baked colours of terracotta and ochre work particularly well in the Mediterranean context where much of life is conducted in the sun: eating, swimming, and relaxing. To my mind, this look would not work elsewhere.

Right This traditional house faces the sea on the Sussex Downs in southeast England, so flint was the correct medium in which to construct the walls with a limestone capping. But since the house is Regency, the style needed to be gracious as well and adapted to the local building medium.

in any pattern? In the temperate north, we have essentially hard or soft woodland, sometimes with lower woodland vegetation (dependent often upon old technique), or open arable land, but with meadow land and marginal wild areas.

The past life of a landscape

If you are in the suburbs, it is still of interest to find out what used to be there, and see what grows in any open spaces nearby. You can then look up the garden form of what grows wild perhaps and use that in your own garden. Undoubtedly some areas are much more distinctive than others. And often as a local you don't recognise it – it takes a stranger's eye. But a clue, I think, can be found by looking at the traditional farming practices of an area – the different crops, different cattle, different building techniques. You can extend this to place names, even field names that you would find on a survey map: they all give a clues to the past life of a landscape.

Above Granite boulders used to create a waterfall in a Scottish garden – totally right in their setting.

Left There is a school of thought that employs shock treatment, contrasting new materials with an old setting. I would defend the right of any designer to try it – after all, it is this 'mix and match' that is often the glory of English architecture. But I believe that it is very difficult to get right. Easier in an urban context, or in limited spaces, say on a roof or balcony, but do have a care in the countryside.

5 I am confused about how to make a pond or how to make a lake. What is the best technique, and where do I go to get help?

John Brookes replies:

There are broadly three techniques for pond building. Clay lining works when you are excavating into clay soil. And this is supplemented with introduced clay (free of stones), which is puddled to create a bowl. One hazard is the water level dropping and the exposed clay cracking. A new technique mixes a fine silicone clay into an existing clay base, sold under the name Bentonite. This sets hard and has so far proved satisfactory.

A butyl rubber liner tends to be expensive, laid over a cushioning layer to avoid stones breaking the butyl from below. Having said that, butyl is pretty tough. A solution has to be found for the edge of the pool: if you want a hard edge the rubber must be laid over a concrete ridge, which adds to the price.

Smaller ponds can use any of these techniques or be built of concrete and/or brick with a waterproof concrete layer inside. Climate and changes in temperature will affect your solution, each has its application.

There are water specialists about who will advise - anywhere selling aquatic plants would know how to locate one. Anthony Archer-Wills, an Englishman living in America, is the author of several excellent books on all these water techniques.

Top right A butyl rubber liner is laid over a permeable layer (sand may be enough). The butyl rubber is then laid over a concrete curb if a sharp edge to the pond is required, and cut off above water line. If a planted edge is needed, rubber is laid over a ledge, to contain earth for planting, and then back into the earth above the water line.

Right This pool has been rubber lined over a concrete block wall, which is faced with timber above the waterline.

6 How do I lay gravel, what gravel do you recommend, and do I lay a permeable layer beneath the gravel?

John Brookes replies:

This is an old chestnut for me. I use a gravel medium to facilitate a loose planting of subjects, which like it hot and dry. I do not therefore need a permeable layer beneath the gravel because I want my plants to self seed into the gravel, and when biennial to overwinter as well. What about the weeds you say - well what about them - get down and start pulling them I say - or use a herbicide. However, I do feel that a dead weed isn't much better than a growing one. Regular raking helps eliminate weed, but don't forget the seedlings you want.

I lay my gravel (crushed flint, a brown colour is my local type), scattered pretty thinly over a layer of unwashed gravel of the same type - hoggin, it's sometimes called. I excavate a few millimetres for this, backfill, role, and sprinkle a fine layer of the clean stuff on top. The finish is hard and easy to walk on - you do not sink in it.

Plant straight into the gravel and its underlayer. Roots will be encouraged to grow downwards, with the gravel on top of them acting as a mulch to prevent water evaporation.

7 Have you ever had any non-payers and if so, what is the procedure?

John Brookes replies

One or two, not many. Lots of slow payers, and that's a hazard if you are on a tight budget. If it is a small amount outstanding you sometimes have to let it go, but once into three figures it's a matter for the Small Claims Court, but the job must be fully documented each step of the way before anyone legal will contemplate it. So it has to be office procedure for every job. Check on whether e-mail, fax, or phone calls are acceptable as business procedures.

Opposite page, far left This gravel garden was constructed in Albany, upstate New York. I was told it would be too hot in summer, and snow would need clearing away in winter. Six years on, it seems to have survived and looks jolly well too. Perennials can self seed in this medium, and their seeds are protected by the gravel in winter. In summer the gravel itself acts as a mulch, retaining moisture in the ground. It helps of course if you plant subjects that like it hot and dry.

Opposite page, left Gravel gardens also work in situations where the soil is thin and fast draining, as it is on chalk downland. Such gardens are not maintenance-free, however. Even if you lay a permeable layer beneath the gravel you will not eliminate weed – for very quickly there is a build up of dust which acts as a growing medium.

Opposite page, right I have no shots of non payers – so here is one of my own garden at Denmans in West Sussex. You can see that even if I am not building a garden, I enjoy putting together plants with structure.

8 Do you go back and visit a job after it is finished being built?

John Brookes replies:

(1) Not unless I am asked, and (2) if I want to photograph it. They pay for (1), (2) you get your photos and they get a free site visit – so check the garden is worth photographing (by looking over the wall), before you ring the bell.

Right and above There is a three-year time span between the planting in this ground floor apartment and the very full effect now.

9 How do you find a reliable contractor to build a garden if you are working in an area you do not know?

John Brookes replies:

First of all, I don't always build. Armed with a detailed plan the client is often happy to supervise or even do the work themselves. Since many of my jobs are at a distance I cannot take on regular supervision.

However, if I was looking for someone in an area I didn't know I would go down to the Society of Garden Designers and ask for a recommendation. Failing that, I would contact the local association of landscape industries, asking them for their members in the area. Alternatively look in the local directories under landscape contractors. Then there is the neighbourhood nursery or garden centre and so on. Once contacted, check the contact out. Ask to see their work – make sure you get on with them, in short: establish a trust whilst going through your drawings with your specifications on site with the contact.

10 What is the right point in the process to consider artificial lighting?

John Brookes replies:

Lighting is now a top 'must have' that clients have begun to demand. I always flippantly say "Let's get something built that's worth lighting first" but they are correct in fact, in that when a structure is about to be built main cables must be laid and recorded, and from which subsequent leads can be taken.

I think that this demand has come about through experiencing warm summer evenings abroad, when one can be outside enjoying balmy nights. Entertaining round the barbecue has further pushed the need for practical lighting, to which increasingly manufacturers are responding with better and better fixtures.

But lighting can be magical in winter too, when from the comfort of your home and with the flick of a switch you can awaken your sleeping garden with a range of lighting effects. Always providing the sleeping garden comes up to snuff when awoken!

Above Lighting can be practical, to light up a path or seating area or to deter intruders, but it can also be an artform, transforming your garden at night or during winter months when natural colour or accent is lacking.

Opposite The strong shapes of the design and the architectural forms of the plant material all help to bring drama into this night-time garden. Water of course, day or night, always becomes a major eyecatcher.

Above Winter spotlighting enlivens the dormant garden.

Opposite Some of the choices available (top to bottom, left to right): uplighting, grazing, washing; cross lighting, accent lighting, silhouetting; mirroring, moonlighting, and spotlighting.

But accenting a single tree or a piece of sculpture may be enough to create visual interest from inside.

Where you do have something worth lighting the next secret is to not overdo it, and to explore all the possibilities. I advise my clients to call in a lighting expert to set up a demonstration since the permutations of what is possible seem endless. Such a demonstration is obviously a night-time operation, and the look will be very different in summer and winter. Frequent adjustments may be necessary as foliage grows.

Then of course security lighting is sensible in certain locations, and safety lighting where you have steps and paving hazards.

In general, garden design can be emphasised at night with pools of light for activity areas, and with a gentle technique to illuminate plant material between them. Ponds and water features can also come into their own.

Most importantly front doors, house names and numbers should be lit adequately. I have listed the sorts of effects that are possible, just so you have the jargon!

Downlighting is obvious, as is **uplighting**, which I prefer.

Grazing is lighting at an acute angle from a close position, to emphasise texture.

Washing (a wall), provides an even coverage of light on a wall to define a space.

Cross lighting is achieved by placing the light to the side of the subject.

Accent lighting uses directional luminaries to emphasise focal points.

Silhouetting is the creation of a dark outline by lighting a surface behind it.

Mirroring is achieved by accent lighting a feature on the far side of water so that its image is mirrored in the dark still water when seen from the house or a terrace.

Moonlighting is a gentle light source down into a tree to create shadow foliage onto the ground below.

Spotlighting is obvious.

Plants may have spreadlighting above them or they may have their outline shadowed onto a wall behind.

Permutations seem endless. And then there are the colours of the lights, and the fixings... Be warned.

Reference

Index

Acknowledgments

I would like first of all to acknowledge the kindness of my clients who have allowed me to use images of their gardens and their garden plans. I thank them. I am all too conscious of not crediting some designers where their agents send unacknowledged material. But where not acknowledged elsewhere, can I also thank: Andy Sturgeon, Martina Barzi and Josefina Casares, James van Sweden and Wolfgang Oehme, Martha Swartz, Tom Stuart-Smith, Steve Martino and Ken Bourke. For other oversights, I apologise.

Everett de Jong and Len Hordyk at Dynascape in Toronto have been most kind in providing their CAD contribution, and I wish them well in launching their product in the UK.

Thanks must go also to artists Nick Bodimeade and Linda Looker for allowing us to reproduce their work.

Lastly, I also would thank Claudia Murphy, who transferred my Luddite hard copy onto computer, Stephanie Evans, who edited it, and Andrew Milne, who laid it all out, so beautifully.

John Brookes, MBE Hon. Doc. Univ. FSGD
Denmans
November 2006

2 Roger Foley: Design Oehme & Van Sweden
8 The Garden Collection/Jonathan Buckley: Design: Christopher Lloyd, Great Dixter
9 John Brookes
10 Nick Bodimeade
11 The Garden Collection/Jonathan Buckley
12 The Garden Collection/Liz Eddison: Design: Andy Sturgeon
13 Roger Foley: Design: Oehme & Van Sweden
14l John Brookes: Design: Martha Swartz
14r Nicola Browne: Design: John Brookes
15tl, tc, tr, cl, br John Brookes
15cl, bl, cr Steven Wooster
16t, b Steve Martino: Design: John Brookes
17t The Garden Collection/Jonathan Buckley: Design: Christopher Lloyd, Great Dixter
17bl The Garden Collection/Gary Rogers
17bcl The Garden Collection/Michelle Garrett
17bcr The Garden Collection/Michelle Garrett
17br The Garden Collection/Gary Rogers
18 The Garden Collection/Marie O'Hara: Design: Earth Designs Ltd
19 Bridgewater Books/Nicola Brown: Design: John Brookes
20 The Garden Collection/Derek Harris
21l The Garden Collection/Liz Eddison: Design: Andy Sturgeon
21r The Garden Collection/Liz Eddison: Design: Fran Forster, Lotus Designs
22tc Corbis/Richard Hamilton Smith
22tl The Garden Collection/Michelle Garrett
22bc Steven Wooster: Design: Tom Stuart-Smith, Chelsea Flower Show 2006
23 Nicola Browne: Design: John Brookes

24l, r John Brookes
25c The Garden Collection/Derek St Romaine
25 John Brookes
26 John Brookes
27t,b John Brookes
28l F G Musashi
28r John Brookes
29 Roger Foley: Design: Oehme & Van Sweden
30 John Brookes
31t, r John Brookes
31br Marilyn & Ken Bourke
32tl The Garden Collection/Michelle Garrett
32tr Roger Foley: Design: Tony Elliott
3cl Nicola Browne
32cr Nicola Browne: Design: Lesley Rosser
32bl, br Angela Copello: Design: Barzi & Casares
33t Linda Looker
33b Marilyn & Ken Bourke
34 Barzi & Casares
35 Roger Foley: Design: Oehme & Van Sweden
36c Corbis/David Zimmerman
36l Corbis/Richard Hamilton Smith
37 Jean Adamson
38 Steven Wooster/Design: Dean Herald, Fleming's Nurseries, Chelsea Flower Show 2006
39t Nicola Browne: Design: John Brookes
39b Tomas Camps
41l Nicola Browne: Design: Sue Berger
41r Steven Wooster: Design: Andy Sturgeon, Chelsea Flower Show 2006
42 Angela Copello: Design: Barzi & Casares
43 Angela Copello: Design: Barzi & Casares
46l John Brookes
46r Martina Barzi: Design: Barzi & Casares

47 Nicola Browne: Design: Pocket Wilson

48 Nicola Browne: Design: Karena Batstone

49t Nicola Browne: Design: Julie Toll

49bl Steven Wooster: Design: Xanthe White, Chelsea Flower Show, 2006

49bc The Garden Collection/Gary Rogers: Design: Giovannella & Carlo Stianti

49br Nicola Browne: Design: Trudy Crevar

50 John Brookes

51l The Garden Collection/Derek Harris

51r John Brookes

52 John Brookes

53 Steven Wooster: Design: Tom Stuart-Smith, Chelsea Flower Show 2006

54tl The Garden Collection/Gary Rogers

54tc Steven Wooster

54tr Alexis Anibal Speron

54cl Nicola Browne: Design: John Brookes

54c, cr, bc, br John Brookes

54bl The Garden Collection/Jonathan Buckley: Design: Roy Day & Steve Harding

55 The Garden Collection/Gary Rogers

56 John Brookes

57tl, tr, b John Brookes

58tl The Garden Collection/Jonathan Buckley: Helen Yemm, Ketley's

58bc Corbis/ Owaki-Kulla

58cr Nicola Browne

59 Gerard Brownstein & Sally Gamble: Design: Ken Bourke

60 John Brookes

61l, r Peter Randall-Page

62t,b John Brookes

63 background Corbis/David Muench

63bl Corbis/O. Alamany & E. Vicens

63bcl Corbis/Dietrich Rose/Zefa

63br Garden Picture Library/Botanica

64t Corbis/Tom Bean

64b The Garden Collection/Gary Rogers

65t Corbis/Owaki-Kulla

65b Corbis/Momatiuk - Eastcott

66 The Garden Collection/Jonathan Buckley: Helen Yemm, Ketley's

67 John Brookes

68tl John Brookes

68bl John Brookes

68tr Corbis /Kit Houghton

68br Corbis/Terry Eggers

69tl Corbis/B.S.P.I

69bl Corbis/Michael S. Yamashita

69tr Corbis/Owen Franken

69br Corbis/Lester Lefkowitz

70t Nicola Browne

70b John Brookes

71tl, cl, bl, John Brookes

71r John Brookes: Design: Marcus Barnett & Phillip Nixon, Chelsea Flower Show 2006

72 John Brookes

73 John Brookes

75tl, tc, tr Bridgewater Books/Nicola Brown: Design: John Brookes

76 Dynascape

77 Bridgewater Books/Nicola Brown: Design: John Brookes

80-1 Dynascape

82 John Brookes

83 John Brookes

84 The Garden Picture Library/Claire Davies

85 The Garden Picture Library/Michael Viard

87 The Garden Picture Library/Botanica

88 Bridgewater Books/Nicola Brown: Design: John Brookes

89 Bridgewater Books/Nicola Brown: Design: John Brookes

90 Bridgewater Books/Nicola Brown: Design: John Brookes

91 John Brookes

92-3 Graham Stroud, Ground Surveys Ltd

96 John Brookes

99 John Brookes

100 John Brookes

101 John Brookes

102 John Brookes

103 John Brookes

104 The Garden Collection/Nicola Stocken Tomkins

105 Lady Egremont

106l The Garden Collection/Derek St Romaine

106r The Garden Picture Library/Linda Burgess

107l Steven Wooster

107r The Garden Collection/Derek Harris

108t The Garden Picture Library/Claire Davies

108b The Garden Picture Library/John Ferro Sims

109t The Garden Picture Library/Eric Crichton

109b The Garden Picture Library/Mark Bolton

110l The Garden Picture Library/Mark Bolton

110r The Garden Collection/Derek St Romaine

111 John Brookes

112 The Garden Picture Library/Juliette Wade

113l The Garden Picture Library/Howard Rice

113c The Garden Picture Library/Suzie Gibbons

113r The Garden Collection/Jonathan Buckley:

Design: Sarah Raven

114l, c, r John Brookes

115tl, tr, bl, br John Brookes

116 John Brookes

118 John Brookes

119 John Brookes

120 Piers Fallowfield Cooper

121 Piers Fallowfield Cooper

122t Bridgewater Books/Nicola Brown: Design: John Brookes

122b Steven Wooster: Design: Xanthe White, Chelsea Flower Show 2006

123 Martina Barzi: Design: Barzi & Casares

124 Bridgewater Books/Nicola Brown: Design: John Brookes

125 Bridgewater Books/Nicola Brown: Design: John Brookes

126 John Brookes

127tc, tr, bl John Brookes

128 Scott Byron & Co

129t, b Scott Byron & Co

130 John Brookes

131 tl, tr, bl, br Scott Byron & Co

132 tr, br John Brookes

133t, bl, br John Brookes

134 Steven Wooster: Design: Xanthe White, Chelsea Flower Show 2006

135 Graham Cartledge

136bl John Brookes

136tr Nicola Browne/Design: John Brookes

137tl, cl, br John Brookes

138t, c, b John Brookes

140c, r John Brookes

141l, r John Brookes

142l, r John Brookes

143 John Brookes

144 John Brookes

146 John Brookes

147l John Brookes

147r Chris Allen

149t, b John Brookes

150 Steven Wooster/Design: Marcus Barnett & Phillip Nixon, Chelsea Flower Show 2006

151 John Brookes/Design: Marcus Barnett & Phillip Nixon, Chelsea Flower Show 2006

152 John Brookes

153 John Brookes

154t, l, r John Brookes

155t, b John Brookes

156t, b, c John Brookes

157 John Brookes

158l, r John Brookes

159 (background) John Brookes

159 br Martina Barzi: Design: Barzi & Casares

160 Nicola Browne/Design: John Brookes

161 John Brookes

162 John Brookes

163t, bl, br Nicola Browne/Design: John Brookes

165t, b John Brookes

166t, tr, cl, br John Brookes

167t Andrew Lawson

167b John Brookes

168l, cl, cr, r John Brookes

169tl, tr, r John Brookes

170 John Brookes,

171 John Brookes

172t, b John Brookes,

173t, b John Brookes

174l, r John Brookes

175 John Brookes

176l, r John Brookes

178l The Garden Collection/Liz Eddison: Design: Ruth Marshall

178c The Garden Collection/Marie O'Hara: Design: Diarmuid Gavin

178r Garden Picture Library/John Swithinbank

179 The Garden Collection/Liz Eddison: Design: Dean Herald, Fleming's Nurseries

180 Garden Picture Library/John Neubauer

181tl The Garden Collection/Liz Eddison

181tc The Garden Picture Library/John Swithinbank

181tr The Garden Picture Library/Steven Wooster

181cl The Garden Collection/Liz Eddison: Design: Diarmuid Gavin

181c The Garden Picture Library/Roger Hyam

181cr The Garden Collection/Liz Eddison: Design: Phil Jaffa

181bl The Garden Collection/Gary Rogers: Design: Alex Daley & Alice Devaney

181bc The Garden Picture Library/Ron Sutherland

181br The Garden Collection/Gary Rogers: Design: Jack Merlo, Fleming's Nurseries.

Mitchell Beazley would like to acknowledge and thank all those who have contributed to this book, and who are credited in the acknowledgments. Every effort has been made to clear copyright but we apologize should any errors or omissions have inadvertently been made.